IDEAS THAT WORK IN COLLEGE TEACHING

Ideas That Work in College Teaching

Edited by

Robert L. Badger

State University of New York Press

Cover photograph © iStockphoto.com / digitalskillet.

Published by
State University of New York Press, Albany

For information, contact State University of New York Press, Albany, NY
www.sunypress.edu

Production, Kelli W. LeRoux
Marketing, Fran Keneston

Library of Congress Cataloging-in-Publication Data

Ideas that work in college teaching / edited by Robert L. Badger.
    p. cm.
  Includes bibliographical references and index.
  ISBN 978–0–7914–7219-4 (hardcover : alk. paper)
  ISBN 978–0–7914–7220–0 (pbk. : alk. paper)
1. College teaching. I. Badger, Robert L.

LB2331.I336 2008
378.1'2—dc22

                                                              2007007846

10 9 8 7 6 5 4 3 2 1

Contents

Foreword

This volume owes its existence to the work of Robert Badger, Professor of Geology at SUNY Potsdam. As he describes in his introduction, after reading several deficient books on the art of teaching, Dr. Badger decided that his colleagues ought to be given a chance to write about what works—and what doesn't work—in college teaching. He knew from numerous conversations that faculty at SUNY Potsdam have thought long and deeply about how they teach, and he suspected that they might have as much to say about teaching as the experts. I think you will find that this volume demonstrates the accuracy of his surmise.

In the booklet that summarizes its policies on reappointment, promotion, and tenure, SUNY Potsdam declares that it "will consider effective teaching as the most important variable" in such deliberations. Members of our faculty actually follow this in their evaluations of their colleagues. It is taken for granted here that teaching is far and away our most important responsibility. And faculties teach a lot, with a teaching load of twelve hours each semester. It's not just that you have to like teaching to stay here very long. If you are to thrive here, teaching must engage you—you must be seriously interested in teaching well, in improving your pedagogy, in learning from mistakes. The people who wrote these essays are thus engaged: devoted to teaching as their primary responsibility, never quite satisfied with their efforts, endlessly fascinated by the ever-changing challenges that the classroom, laboratory, and studio present.

Another feature of SUNY Potsdam faculty that encourages discussions of pedagogy is their passion for interdisciplinary work. Each semester's offerings contain many learning communities of two to five courses with common enrollment, focused on a common theme. First-year students are unable to escape one or more Freshman Interest Groups, which are course clusters specifically designed to help beginning college students investigate an area of study. These cooperative teaching activities put faculty of different disciplines in close contact with one another and compel discussions about how to present material so that it will be of most use to the interdisciplinary dialogue. The chapters in this book manifest the comprehensive view of the teaching enterprise that emerges from this kind of shared endeavor.

Our School of Education and Professional Studies has as a primary goal that its graduates shall be "reflective practitioners" as they practice the teaching profession. I think this is a worthy goal for teachers at all levels. May we learn to be reflective as we practice our craft, and may we turn that reflection to good effect in our conduct of our classes and laboratories and studios. The chapters in this book are evidence of pedagogic reflection by teachers at this college. We present them in the hope that they may be helpful, even inspirational, to all scholars who care deeply about their teaching, wherever they may be.

Galen K. Pletcher
Dean of Arts and Sciences
Professor of Philosophy

Preface

Behind the Making of this Book

The day that I conceived of this project, my environmental geology students and I met at a local cemetery to study the effects of acid rain on the different types of tombstones. As the students arrived, I handed out their assignments, carefully spelled out. Most students took the sheet of paper and began to read. One student, however, accepted the directions, thanked me, stuffed them into his backpack, then looked up and asked, in complete innocence, "What are we supposed to do here?"

The day before, my students in structural geology had an assignment due. This project involved the use of a microscope and, once I got them started, they needed no further instruction. We had started in class on Tuesday, but, when time ran out, I asked them to finish on their own and hand in the assignment at the beginning of Thursday's class. I emphasized *beginning* of class, Thursday *morning*, as the class meets again for a lab on Thursday afternoon. Some students had been less than diligent in meeting deadlines, so I looked several right in the eye and queried their listening capabilities. "Ryan, Thursday morning?" "Friday afternoon," he joked, "no problem." Turning to another student, "James? Thursday morning?" He nodded. "Michael?" "That soon?" was his reply. "Yes, Thursday, *morning*," was my emphatic response. Thursday morning rolled around, and only eight of the twelve had the assignment completed. Surprisingly, Ryan's was finished, but James skipped class, two others that I hadn't looked right in the eye were still incomplete, and Michael said, "Oh, I thought you meant Thursday afternoon for lab."

I'm sure something equally inane happened the day before, and several times the previous week, and the week before, and the week before that. Every contributor to this volume encounters the same frustrations, and I am certain that everyone reading these words can relate. Many days I leave school shaking my head, wondering what am I doing here, why am I teaching these... these... (several words come to mind).

A few years ago, I had a class at the Blue Mountain Lake Museum, an outdoor museum deep in the Adirondacks. The museum consists of over two dozen display buildings, each devoted to some aspect of life in the early days of civilization in the mountains—logging, mining, recreation, art, transportation, the great camps, and so on. At one point, a student reported that four other students had scaled the fence and left the compound. Hmmm. This wasn't a prison; it has a front entranceway and an exit—why scale the fence? When she told me which four, I was sure they had jumped ship to smoke a joint, and when I went to investigate, I found them climbing back in. "Why do I have to deal with this crap," I remembered thinking at the time. My role is not as prison guard, camp counselor, or even babysitter. I am supposed to be teaching college students, motivating them to learn, piquing their intellectual excitement. Three of those students dropped or flunked out of school before the end of the year. The fourth became an honors student and presidential scholar. When he graduated three years later, he sent me a card and a note thanking me for being a mentor and role model, saying, "You are part of who I am today."

Last year a graduating senior presented me with a small rock sample consisting of a clump of clear to milky quartz embedded with several dark green, inch-long bladed crystals of the mineral arfvedsonite. We had briefly encountered this mineral during laboratory in a senior-level geology class. One of the goals of the course is for students to make connections between what they see microscopically and megascopically in a rock hand sample. Arfvedsonite is quite rare, and our department's mineral collection, though very good, did not include a sample. So when the student spotted a sample at a gem and mineral show, he bought it, and at the end of the year presented it to me with a note thanking me for an excellent course.

Not long ago I received the following email from a recent graduate:

Dr. Badger,
I want to thank you and the rest of the geology staff for having an excellent geology program. The quality of the program and the teaching methods used were top-notch.... I have recently accepted a position with Scientific Laboratories Inc. as a polarized light microscopist.... I don't think I would have landed this position if it weren't for Optics and Mineralogy. Once again, thank you for a great education.

These students provide the impetus for why I teach: the ones who jump the fence, but come back; the ones who make connections; the ones who get motivated and somehow make us feel that we were part of that motivation. Was it something I did? Something I said? How did I connect to one student, but not to another in the same class? Why was my colleague in anthropology successful at motivating a particular student while I was not? What did she do that worked? To that end, I hope that this book will contain some ideas that others can use or adapt to their own teaching situations to help students learn, to motivate them, or to help some of them back over the fence.

Our last provost started an informal book discussion series, which our current provost recognized as a good idea and continued.* It involved reading one book each semester, purely voluntary. We read, or (perhaps emulating our students) skim through, then meet on a Friday afternoon with a few bottles of wine. Usually we begin with a panel discussion, followed by a general discussion. The books always focus on education methods, reform, philosophy, or some such topic, and are the provost's gentle and subtle (yet effective) way of encouraging us to keep looking for new ways to teach, for new ideas to bring to the classroom. Each semester's panel consists of a group of faculty selected by the provost from diverse fields in our institution. For one semester the panel consisted of members of the psychology, education, and communication departments. For another, a sociologist teamed with a geologist, historian, and musician; another panel consisted of a physicist with an anthropologist, photographer, and English professor. Generally, we have no big egos (little ones, perhaps); we have mutual respect for our colleagues' disciplines and are wholly supportive of one another in our teaching endeavors. So these interdisciplinary panels work well, particularly if the wine is flowing freely.

Although there have been one or two mildly heated arguments, and perhaps a few blood pressures raised, no blood has been shed, no noses broken, and as far as I know, no egos bruised. We have read some thought-provoking books: *Consilience* by Edward O. Wilson; *How Nature Works* by Per Bak; *Punished by Rewards* by Alfie Kohn; *Rethinking Liberal Education*, edited by Farnham and Yarmolinsky. These have led to good discussions, and most of us have come away with something tangible and a feeling that the afternoon was time well spent.

---

*I should note that Provost Peter Brouwer, who initiated the series, has returned to our academic ranks and contributed chapter 5.

However, we have been less than enamored with a couple of books. One was branded as pure psychobabble by a science faculty member, whose comments were preceded by a sociologist who admitted to being thoroughly embarrassed to find the author of such diatribe was also a sociologist. Most of us rather enjoyed lambasting it, and came away feeling that, too, was a worthwhile endeavor.

Another book prompted a member of our Politics Department to write a three page document that he read to the audience, expressing his anger and indignation toward a writer who to him seemed like a spoiled, whining brat. We almost unanimously concurred. The author droned on and on, complaining about her students, who were from some of the finest Division I colleges in the country. As our discussion wound down, the moderator asked if there was anyone who had not yet spoken who would like to get in a word. That was my cue. I strolled to the front of the room, delivered my own editorial comment that far too many trees had been sacrificed to print such drivel, and voiced the opinion that we could do better.

The attendant faculty group represented most of the seventeen departments in our school of Arts and Sciences, plus members from our School of Education and the Crane School of Music. Indeed, before me was a fine cross section of the university faculty, and, just by their presence, all were interested in teaching and learning. Many, I knew, did interesting things in their classrooms from which we all could learn. "John, you teach a really unique course in politics. Can you write about it? Kim, I know you do wonderful things in Drama to motivate your students. Caroline, I've been in your art classes and seen how you can get the artistically challenged to draw. David, students rave about your Philosophy classes; you must do something right."

I received several nods, and mumbles of approval. I continued rambling, "Our students aren't born with a silver spoon in their mouths and sent off to the elite colleges of the country. We're not Division I; we're Division III." At which point I heard a "Hear, Hear" from a politics professor in the front row. Many of our students are the first generation of their family to attend college. Their parents are farmers, truck drivers, mechanics, construction workers. Some students have no parental support to attend college, and 80 percent receive financial aid. But if our van breaks down while on a class field trip, they don't pull out their AAA card and cell phone; they pop the hood open and try to figure out what's wrong. If a piece of lab equipment breaks down and a replacement part is available, they will retrieve their toolbox and do the job themselves, instead of complaining that the equipment is broken. These are generally really good kids but, for most of them, education has been neither a top personal nor a family priority, and therein lies our challenge.

We're starting with pretty raw material. For those who really are freshmen, just out of high school, they are also freshmen in life. Their only travel out of state may have been a family vacation when they were in grade school, or trips to visit a relative in a nearby state. Work experience has been on the family farm, at a fast food restaurant, at a meatpacking plant, or doing odd jobs around the community. A fair number are older students. Some failed miserably when they first attended college at age eighteen, but now, five or ten years later, are ready to try again, this time better prepared psychologically. Some were in the military. Some have small children, and when the local schools are closed for a snow day, our classrooms sometimes resemble daycare centers. This is the typical clientele for many state schools—good kids, fine people, but often ill-prepared for immersion into academia.

So I put forth the challenge to my fellow faculty: Let's write about our own experiences, our many perspectives for the same target group of students. This is not the norm for this type of book. More commonly, contributors to edited collections of educational works are from a wide range of institutions with disparate student populations. Many are universities with extensive graduate programs. Often the authors are administrators, education specialists, and researchers. Our goal was different. As members of the faculty of the same college, the State University of New York College at Potsdam, we have the same pool of students. Our intent was to show how professors of psychology, biology, teacher education, and all the others approach this group from within our respective disciplines.

Several faculty accepted the challenge immediately and enthusiastically. I did a little arm-twisting and others slowly came on board, until we eventually had twenty who gave me a definite "maybe." Of these, finished chapters were received from fifteen, representing thirteen different disciplines of study: art, biology, computer science, education, geology, history, math, modern languages, philosophy, physics, politics, psychology, and sociology. These fifteen chapters offer ideas and philosophies that we have found successful. The basic theme is to try whatever works. Nothing works for all students; nearly everything works for at least a few. Our goal is to maximize our efforts. To that end, all of these stories and ideas are really not discipline specific. A concept that works in physics perhaps can be modified to work in philosophy; a teaching method used in history may be transferable to math.

In our case, service learning, a concept well explained by sociology professor Heather Sullivan-Catlin in chapter 2, is relevant to any discipline. In chapter 12, physics professor Larry Brehm suggests passing out office coupons that the student must redeem within a set time period by visiting the professor in his or her office. This idea can be used in any discipline to forge better student/teacher relationships. Professor Brehm also suggests not creating homework problems until after class ends, thereby allowing for the design of problems that pertain directly to what was done in class, and then sending the homework to students by email or Blackboard posting. Why didn't I think of this? Too many times in my teaching career I have designed a homework assignment, only to have to modify my directions when handing it out: "Only do problems one and two. You'll have to wait until next class to learn how to do three and four."

I hope you enjoy these chapters and perhaps come away with some useful new idea or concept. Some chapters are lighthearted, written in an informal style with ideas based on anecdotal evidence; others are written in a more formal research article mode. I set no prepublication format. Even if I had, my colleagues probably would have ignored me. If one style bothers you, or you find the subject matter not particularly relevant to your discipline, skip it and move on to the next. There is no direct connection between the chapters, and there is no rhyme or reason to their sequencing. I briefly struggled to impose some sequence that made sense. Finding none, I just pulled them out of my "Ed Book Final" folder in whatever order the computer had haphazardly arranged them. My only tweaking was to separate computer science from math, and to pair the two (art and geology) that referred to our Adirondack Studies Program.

My undergraduate mentor, Brew Baldwin at Middlebury College, had an office door plastered with cartoons and quotes. One of my favorites was labeled "The Gerber Model of Education: One way to feed strained food to a baby is to use a baby spoon and get 'the airplane to go into the hangar.' This is very neat and precise. The other way is to use a butter knife to move the food from one cheek to the other; in each pass, some food gets into the mouth." We don't want to spoon-feed our students, so I guess we are all using butter knives. These pages discuss our attempts to teach our students to lick their lips.

Robert Badger

1

There Is No Such Thing as a Dumb Student, But How Can I Help Them Do Better?

Joel Foisy
Mathematics Department

I try to take an honest look at my own development as a teacher, and how my experience working with students at SUNY Potsdam has shaped that development. Starting with the premise that I want students to learn some mathematics, to improve their logical thinking and communication skills, and enjoy the process, I explore how this can best be achieved. Getting students to see ideas in a variety of ways, to reflect on concepts, to explain concepts to their peers orally and to me in writing is the best way to achieve this goal, though different classes and different students respond to a variety of techniques. In mathematics, students also need encouragement and motivation to stick with a technically and creatively demanding subject.

One of my all-time favorite lessons involves showing that the "dual" of a cube is an octahedron. To get the dual of a solid, you place a vertex in each face of the solid, and connect vertices of adjacent faces with an edge. Got it? To illustrate this, I brought in some tape and string. The cube in question was our classroom. One of our taller students volunteered to place a vertex in the center of each wall (tape the string down). As a result, we had a room-sized cube with a room-sized octahedron made out of string (the octahedron has six corners, twelve edges, and eight faces). On their way out of the classroom, students had to be careful not to get caught in the web of this octahedron. During the next class my tall volunteer could not recall what the dual of the cube is. I felt discouraged. Wasn't this a great lesson plan? Then a few months later, at graduation, I ran into another student from this same course. She excitedly told me that she had used this same lesson in her elementary school student teaching, with great success. This experience has led to perhaps my biggest teaching lesson: what we do in the same class can be soon forgotten by one student, yet have a profound impact on another. To ensure that we reach the largest possible cross section of learners, we must use a variety of classroom approaches. We must somehow let students know their learning and development are important to us, we must motivate them to want to learn, and we must review important themes.

CONTEXT FOR SUCCESS: SHOWING STUDENTS YOU CARE ABOUT THEIR LEARNING

My father taught mathematics at SUNY Potsdam (it was called Potsdam State in those days) while I was growing up. By nearly all accounts, he was an amazingly successful teacher. From what I can remember about his dinner table conversations concerning work, one consistent theme emerged. He loved talking about students—where they were from, what they were going into, how he had taught so-and-so's parents, how they had done well, and so on. Recently, a graduate from the late sixties came to campus to give a talk. My father could recall the names of more of the alumnus's friends than the alum could. Although learning mathematics was the basis of his interactions with students, and my father did like the subject he taught, he clearly cared about his students much more than the mathematics itself.

I have appreciated the supportive environment I have had since joining the faculty at Potsdam; my department has shown confidence in me, which has helped me grow professionally. Similarly, teachers need to show confidence in our students, so that they may grow academically and as people. When students are struggling with math problems, we need to listen to their approach (and possibly encourage them to develop an approach, even if that approach is not directly leading them to a correct answer), then help guide them toward their own understanding of the material, getting in the way as little as possible.

In college, I became a mathematics major partly because the only courses I got A's in were math courses, partly because there were many excellent professors in the math department, and partly because the math department at my school offered a free meal to any student who declared a major in mathematics. I cannot underestimate the importance of that meal. As a student, it was so nice to have a department make a gesture of appreciation (economics and political science made no such gesture—they had enough majors already and did not need to recruit). As a teacher, I take away from this experience one key concept: students love food. For the past two springs, I have held a dinner at my house for math majors. About twenty-five students show up every year, along with a good number of faculty, and it has been a great time. My department also recognizes outstanding students by inducting them into an honor society and offering summer research opportunities. Showing respect and kindness can go a long way in motivating students.

How Testing and Assessment Can Help Students

I also believe that it is important to be tough. I can summarize my philosophy: keep standards high, but be flexible. At SUNY Potsdam, some of our students are not confident and resilient enough to accept the challenge of a bluntly demanding teacher. When I was a first year student, I remember getting a terrible grade on a certain assignment. This only prompted me to work even harder (and I was already putting forth a substantial effort). I talked about this sort of policy—grading hard on the first paper—with my colleague Blair Madore. He responded that such a policy may work well at a highly selective school where the students are more eager to be challenged, but he was not sure how successful it would be at Potsdam. He suggested grading gently at first and then gradually easing into a more demanding fashion. This keeps the students engaged without demeaning them, and is ultimately demanding. In practice, I must admit that I have found it difficult to make the transition into stricter grading.

It has been the philosophy of the mathematics department that helping students understand concepts in depth is more important for student intellectual development than "covering" a lot of material. Helping them learn how to think logically and develop intellectually is paramount. To keep the students engaged, we need to offer tasks that are challenging, but ones they can do. This means giving them challenging tests, but not so difficult that they are thrown into a panic or feel demeaned. Writing a good test requires walking a fine line. If you consider that there are usually about thirty students in the class, this makes constructing a good test even more difficult. Ideally, we as teachers must strike a balance between creating a comfortable and welcoming environment in the classroom, while being cognizant of the reality that learning is difficult and that students sometimes need to be prodded to put forth the effort they need to master the subject material.

DAY-TO-DAY IN THE CLASSROOM

I believe that lecturing can be an effective way to teach, especially if it is done in an interactive manner. I also believe, however, that following the same routine every day can make students feel too comfortable and unmotivated. I thus try to assign a nonlecture-focused project at least every couple of weeks, especially in calculus. Though there are an abundance of projects commercially available, very few appeal to me as appropriate; most are either too boring or too impossible. In particular, projects that have students work on real-world application problems can get quite messy. They are of limited direct benefit because, frankly, most students will not do applied mathematics for a living. In life after school, most students will need to be able to think logically to help a business or to write a computer program, and such logic can be best learned through the study of pure mathematics. In keeping with my department's philosophy, an ideal project does not make students feel overwhelmed, yet it stretches their thinking and forces them to work together to succeed.

Writing an appropriate level project is time consuming and requires creativity; however, there are a few that I like. Every differential equations book discusses Newton's Law of Cooling—a way to estimate how long a body has been cooling based on a couple of temperature readings at different times. A popular application of this is to figure out when a person died. I have had students work on a mock trial that uses Newton's Law of Cooling as the main evidence. A student is accused of murdering his or her professor from the previous semester. Students must then form defense, prosecution, and media teams. The students have to present mathematical arguments in court to either establish or throw in doubt the time of death. The last time I did this activity, George Kahn, our local audiovisual expert, filmed the mock trial. George was a great asset to the project. He provided pretrial music (Bach's Toccata and Fugue), and borrowed a graduation robe for me so that I could look like a proper judge. I invited some high-level administrators to the case, and instructed the students to take their job seriously. Most of the presentations went smoothly, although one student made a mathematical mistake that the provost noticed. Of course, we discussed the student's mistake during the next class, and I'm sure that the experience of participating in the trial heightened the student's interest in understanding the mistake. This was an event I will never forget.

I should point out that as a result of the mock trial project, we ended up spending a couple of extra class days on Newton's Law of Cooling (and, to be honest, it is not the most difficult topic in the course). Thus, for reasons of time, I am only able to do one such project per semester. I believe that good projects can add a lot to the students' classroom experience, but these projects are difficult to find, and they are time consuming.

INTERACTING WITH STUDENTS

My father has taught me that the preparation you do outside of class is not nearly as important as how you interact with students in the classroom. One of his primary vehicles for interaction was using 3 x 5 index cards. Each card included an individual student's name and some information about the student. He used to shuffle the cards, fire questions to his class, and randomly call on students to answer them. This does keep students alert. He would lecture very little, perhaps the last fifteen minutes of class. More than one alumnus has told me that my father could sniff out whether they had done their homework, and that he could make them want to complete their homework for the next class. I have heard from his colleagues that students would not like my father's courses for the first half of the semester or so, but were won over by the end. He was tough on them, but at the same time obviously cared about them and their learning of the subject.

I have used the random card technique with some success. On the end-of-semester evaluations, many students have said that it keeps them on their toes, and very few have complained about feeling put out by having to speak out in class. By calling on everyone, students tend to feel more comfortable speaking up when it is their turn. I did have one faculty observer say that he believed such a random calling system was bound to make some introverted students feel uncomfortable. In retrospect, there was always a student or two in every class whom I would not call on even if their card came up (or, more precisely, I would only call on them once). I still use 3 x 5 cards, but have also tried other techniques, like having students explain a concept to their neighbor (and thus the shy ones need not speak out in front of the entire class). Generally, this technique is effective, but it does not always work perfectly. Sometimes the class is reduced to silence. When this happens, I momentarily leave the room and instruct the students to talk to each other; this usually works. Or I tell them that if the silence continues, I will call on one of them to explain what is going on to the rest of the class. Another technique is simply to have students write down their explanation to a given question.

When a student asks a question, I often do not answer it directly myself; instead I give the rest of the students in the class the chance to answer. That way the students feel ownership of the course. I also try not to repeat what a student says verbatim, although I may try to paraphrase what they say. This allows the students to feel they have a voice in the class. It is not always best for our students to give an immediate answer to their question. Usually, they need time to figure things out for themselves. On the flip side, sometimes we can be too evasive in answering their questions, creating excessive frustration and loss of confidence on their part. Finding a balance is not easy, and depends on the particular student in question.

I enjoy having students work on homework problems at the board. Doing so gives me immediate feedback as to how they are progressing and forces a good portion of the students to explain their work and assume an active role in the classroom. Having said this, sending students to the board can create difficulties because they always take up more time working on problems than I anticipate. Consequently, I currently do not send students to the board more frequently than once a week.

Often while students are working on a project, I will interrupt their group work and talk at the blackboard for five minutes about a question that has come up for several groups. At these times, the students are primed to pay attention and digest what I say. Similarly, when I am "lecturing," I will frequently interrupt the class to have them work on a question (the lecture is interrupted by a project). In addition, I often stop the class and say that we will not progress until someone asks a question. An uncomfortable pause usually ensues, but then inevitably someone will speak up. I always try to circulate in the classroom, getting in the students' space. I believe this makes me seem more accessible, and it makes the class just a little more exciting (especially after I trip over a desk trying to walk between rows).

I do not believe that students have to reconstruct mathematics for them to understand it, although I would not rule this out as a good way to learn. I do believe that they have to internalize the material at hand; they must make it their own. To do so, they need to work on the material, and they need to be able to talk through the course content (which is a theme in *Thinking About Teaching and Learning* by Robert

Leamnson). Our interactions with students must force them to explain the material in class, ask questions, and motivate them to work on the material outside of class.

QUICK ACTIVITIES

There is an abundance of quick activities and demonstrations one can do to make students more interested, and I am always on the lookout for such activities. Jokes are a classic way to get students to pay more attention. In third semester calculus, I always ask the students what results from crossing a dog with a cat. The answer, of course, is (dog)(cat)(sin theta)(n). The next question is what results from crossing a dog with a goat. The answer is that you cannot cross a dog and a goat because the goat is a scalar. The students groan at these, but they appreciate the effort, and maybe, just maybe, it will help them remember the definition of the cross product of two vectors. (If anyone knows any good math jokes, please email me.)

When I discuss angles and angle measure in the beginning of calculus, I review it with the students by having them stand up and make the angles with their own arms. This does not take very long, and it is my hope that it helps some of the more kinesthetic students remember what an angle measuring pi radians looks like in standard position. I also get immediate visual feedback as to how well the students understand angles.

By definition, quick activities are quick; they are ad hoc. I try to use them whenever possible. Anything that breaks the routine and either gets the students' attention or forces them to think about the subject is useful.

CROSS-CURRICULAR CONNECTIONS

Cross-curricular connections are always effective, and do not necessarily require much effort. In calculus, connections to physics are easily made. When we discuss modeling the height of a dropping ball, we use a CBL (calculus based laboratory) system that will plot the height of an actual dropped ball over time. It does not take very long to drop the ball and it shows some practical minded students that the functions we are studying do relate to physical reality. In third-semester calculus, much of the end of the semester is difficult for students, particularly Green's theorem. I have taught this course often and only this past time did I make a conscious effort to point out that what we do is directly related to physics and electrostatics. I must confess that I did not mention physics connections because I was not comfortable with the physics since I had never taken a college-level course in it. This past year, I asked one of my colleagues from the physics department for a spare physics book and quickly read it. At the end of the semester, students commented on their evaluation forms on how much they appreciated how the course related to physics.

I have had the privilege of teaching a math for liberal arts students course. In such a course, there are ample opportunities for discussing how math relates to other topics. I used the book *The Heart of Mathematics* by Burger and Starbird, which discusses many connections to art, music, and science. We did classic activities, like measure angles of triangles on a globe, construct Mobius strips, and then cut them up. We discussed the golden ratio and how composer Claude Debussy used it in his musical work "Prelude to the Afternoon of a Faun," and even listened to the piece in class for a couple of minutes. Several music majors in the class appreciated this activity, and it was simple and quick. When we studied fractals, I brought in my Oliver Schroer avant-garde CD of "fractal reels." His music was inspired by geometric fractals. I wish every mathematical topic had such great musical accompaniment. It is not always easy to make connections to other disciplines, but it is well worth the effort.

SUMMARY

My main goal is getting students to think for themselves, while learning the subject matter at hand. There is no one way to achieve this; any given class is really many different classes—one for each student involved. Even what we think are excellent classroom activities will not have a serious impact on all the students in the class. This is why I try to vary my technique, and also to respond to the individual class, and the individuals in the class, as much as possible. I hope that after a semester with me, students become more enthusiastic for the subject, remember some of the important themes of the course, and want to learn more.

REFERENCES

Burger, E., and M. Starbird. *The Heart of Mathematics*. Emeryville, CA: Key College Publishing, 2000.
Leamnson, Robert. *Thinking about Teaching and Learning*. Virginia: Stylus Publishing, 1999.

2

Service Learning in Sociology: Replacing Hopelessness with Efficacy

Heather Sullivan-Catlin
Department of Sociology

> People who like to avoid shocking discoveries, who prefer to believe that society is just what they were taught in Sunday School, who like the safety of the rules and maxims of...the world taken for granted should stay away from sociology.
> —Peter Berger, *Invitation to Sociology*

I became a sociologist for the same reason that many of my colleagues have pursued this discipline: to change the world. More specifically, we pursue sociology to understand social problems in order to help solve them. As a result, teaching our discipline can often be an exercise in consciousness-raising and students often learn the lesson alluded to by Peter Berger: sociology can shake you up.

Indeed, learning sociology is about developing a new way of looking at the world. C. Wright Mills (1959) called it "the sociological imagination"—a lens that enables us to see the relationship between individual experiences and larger social and historical forces. Developing one's ability to uncover the systemic roots of problems that society often attributes to personal failures (such as poverty) can be

9

unsettling and often leads to a sense of hopelessness. But rather than leave them depressed, I hope to inspire students to take action. Service learning can help students develop a sense of efficacy while providing them with the tools to become engaged citizens (Eyler and Giles, 1999; Hironimus-Wendt and Lovell-Troy, 1999; Myers-Lipton, 1998; Sullivan-Catlin, 2002). I will describe here my use of service learning in the introductory sociology course, beginning with a brief introduction to service learning pedagogy and its applicability to the teaching of sociology at my university.

Service Learning

The field of sociology is extremely broad, but a central theme is that there is a structure to social groups—groups as small as families and as large as entire societies—and that structure influences the experiences of every individual in the group. However, as Howery has argued, "social structure cannot be seen, and thus students learning about it must experience directly or indirectly its dimensions. Service learning provides that opportunity to see how social location shapes so much of what occurs in our individual and collective experiences" (1999, 152).

In a service learning class, students are engaged in course-related community work. The community service activity is specifically designed to meet a need articulated by the community *and* to provide students with an experience that will enhance their learning of the curriculum. Here are some examples:

- Students in a criminology class tutoring inmates in a nearby correctional facility.
- Research methods students conducting a family needs assessment survey for a local Head Start program.
- A class on gender creating public awareness materials (e.g., brochures, posters, etc.) for a community domestic violence program.
- Students in a class on race and ethnicity developing and presenting a diversity workshop for the local elementary school.

Simply assigning a service activity in a course will not, however, automatically result in enhanced student learning. Effective service learning pedagogy requires that the service experience be brought back into the classroom. Students need to reflect on the service activities and be encouraged to make the connections between their experiences and the concepts they have learned in readings, lectures, and other course materials. These reflective and integrative processes can be facilitated through journals, class discussion, papers, and even exams. The effectiveness of this approach for teaching sociology has been well documented (see Mooney and Edwards, 2001; Ostrow, Hesser, and Enos, 1999; Teaching Sociology 1998).

Service learning can be used in any discipline in any institutional setting, but is especially applicable to teaching sociology at SUNY Potsdam. Recent institutional assessments have revealed that too few entering students have confidence in their intellectual and social capabilities and recent surveys tell us that our students are less invested in their educational experience than the norm (SUNY Potsdam, 2000). However, surveys of incoming first-years found that 83.6 percent of our students have performed volunteer work and 29 percent indicate that they will likely participate in service during their college career, making service the highest ranked of anticipated college activities (CIRP, 2001).

While community service itself has many potential positive outcomes, Myers-Lipton has shown that students involved in a comprehensive service-learning program "show larger increases in civic responsibility when compared to students involved in community service but who are not formally integrating it with their academic course work" (1998, 243). Service learning takes community involvement from *extra*curricular to being integrated into the curriculum.

As for my goal of replacing student hopelessness with a sense of efficacy, there is strong evidence that service learning is an excellent way to achieve it. According to Eyler, Giles, Stenson, and Gray (2001), service learning's student outcomes include:

- Positive effects on students' academic learning, including increased motivation to learn and deeper understanding of subject matter.
- Improvement in students' ability to apply what they have learned in "the real world."
- Positive effects on student personal development including their sense of personal efficacy, personal identity, and moral development.
- Positive effects on interpersonal development, the ability to work well with others, leadership and communication skills.
- Positive effects on reducing stereotypes and facilitating cultural and racial understanding.
- Positive effect on sense of social responsibility and citizenship skills and commitment to service.

These outcomes would be welcome in any classroom and I have designed my Sociology 101 course with them in mind.

SOCIOLOGY 101

The purpose of Sociology 101 is to introduce the key concepts, main theoretical perspectives, and basic research methods of sociology. I commit a great deal of energy and time to teaching this course because I see it as one of the most important courses offered by my department. Its importance is based on two factors. First, Sociology 101 fulfills a "general education" requirement, so it reaches many students outside of the major. Second, it is the main point of entry into the major. Students are rarely exposed to sociology in high school and consequently relatively few enter college with a sociology major in mind.

In order to integrate service learning into the course, I have adopted a theme: *food, hunger, and poverty.* We use this topic as the foundation for many of our class activities and assignments. The service sites and projects reflect this theme as well. Our primary community partner (the term for community agencies in service learning) is the Potsdam Neighborhood Center, which offers several emergency food programs to low-income community members. This small organization relies heavily on volunteer labor, coordinated by the director, who is the only full-time paid staff person. Student activities at the neighborhood center include unloading food deliveries, sorting donated food in the pantry, and assisting with food distributions. Food distributions occur several times a year when the regional food bank delivers a truckload of food to be distributed in one day. Students help unload the truck, organize the food, check recipients in to collect demographic data and verify income eligibility, and assist recipients with gathering various food items. This activity allows for extensive interaction with other volunteers (primarily local retirees) and direct interaction with food recipients.

I have found that working with one primary community partner is a very effective service-learning practice. It allows the class to focus on the shared service experience and to explore the specific issues raised by our involvement at a particular site. However, the Neighborhood Center's hours are not always suitable for every student's schedule and I offer several other options in keeping with community needs and the course theme. These include Meals on Wheels, Head Start, and community suppers at local churches.

Through the service-learning experiences, students learn how to apply a sociological perspective when observing and participating in the social world. However, this does not just happen automatically. Indeed, left unexamined, service-learning experiences have the potential to backfire (*reinforcing* rather than dispelling stereotypes). Linkages must be made between the theoretical and the experiential. If students come away from the course wondering why they were required to engage in community service, the two have not been well connected. The service experience in the wider community *can* help bring to life major course concepts (including the structure of society, culture, socialization, social stratification, social change, and so on), but faculty must help students make those connections.

Integrating Service with Learning

I integrate the field experience with the course curriculum through a variety of methods, including texts, lectures, reflective writing, group discussion, field trips, homework activities, and essay exams.

I began teaching this course several years ago in a very traditional fashion—without service learning and with a basic textbook and reader. I found that students regularly ignored the reading or complained that the text was too boring. I was also reluctant to continue with this approach, as I found it too broad. Over a fifteen-week semester I would cover over a dozen chapters/topics, resulting in a course with great breadth, but lacking depth.

As I have incorporated service learning and developed the course, I have switched to using a combination of texts. They have included full-length monographs, policy- and data-oriented booklets, and topical narrative texts. They are chosen for their coverage of a variety of sociological concepts as well as their application to the service-learning component. Initially I required a total of six texts, but students found this to be burdensome and I have adjusted accordingly. I currently use four books:

- *The Forest and The Trees: Sociology As Life, Practice & Promise* (Allan G. Johnson, 1997, Temple University Press)
- *Freedom Summer* (Doug McAdam, 1988, Oxford University Press)
- *Sweet Charity? Emergency Food and the End of Entitlement* (Janet Poppendieck, 1998, Penguin Books)
- *The Call of Service: A Witness to Idealism* (Robert Coles, 1993, Houghton Mifflin)

While this amount of reading still challenges the students, I find they often rise to my expectations. These texts help tie sociology to service learning, but Poppendieck's *Sweet Charity* is particularly useful in this regard. I use it to illustrate a variety of sociological topics and concepts, including research methods, theory, stratification, institutionalization, social change, and social movements. While service learning can help increase efficacy, it can also lead to complacency and reinforce the idea that individual service and a "thousand points of light" are the answer to systemic social problems. *Sweet Charity* helps us examine the limits of charity and volunteerism for solving social problems and creating social change.

In addition to my choice of texts, I integrate service with learning in each aspect of the course. When I present a lecture on a new topic, I illustrate the concepts with local examples or encourage students to find connections to their experience. For example, when teaching the concept of *resocialization* (the process of socializing people into new cultures and environments, like a new job) I ask students how they are oriented to (or *resocialized into*) the community setting. One of the answers is our class field trip to the Potsdam Neighborhood Center. The trip occurs early in the semester and introduces students to the staff, the organization, and the issues of hunger and poverty in our community.

Much of the integration of service and learning happens outside class. Students keep journals in which they record their experiences and also respond to questions and readings (especially Coles's *The Call of Service*). Reflective writing is not limited to journals, though. The course's midterm and final exams are take-home essay exams that include questions asking students to incorporate readings, class activities, and service experiences. For example, one question on the final reads:

> According to Johnson and the sociological perspective, "if you're not part of the solution, you're part of the problem." Coles tells of the many people he has encountered and what he learned about service from them. Over the course of this semester you have come into contact with many new people in the context of the service-learning project. Describe one of these people and how they are "part of the solution."

Finally, homework assignments give students another opportunity to connect course materials and service experiences while learning skills for community involvement. One such assignment asks students to write a letter to one of their elected representatives. This can be an elected official at any level: local (village, town, city, county) official; state senator, assemblyperson or governor; national senator or house representative; or the president. The goal of the letter is to urge action on the part of their representative. It can be related to any "food, hunger, poverty" issue the student feels strongly about. Students enjoy this assignment. Many report that it demystifies the process of contacting an elected representative and comment that they are likely to do so again in the future.

Overcoming Student Resistance

The service-learning requirement often takes students by surprise and they occasionally offer resistance. Why? Despite the rise of service learning in K–12 education, a large majority of my students have never experienced this kind of active learning. They expect to read textbooks, be lectured to, and take tests. Many of my colleagues have also encountered resistance in their attempts to incorporate more participatory learning strategies into their classes. For example, in chapter 14 Peg Wesselink writes, "It sometimes feels as though we are dragging our students kicking and screaming into participating in their own education rather than integrating them into a liberating educational experience."

One of my strategies for addressing this resistance is to share writings that deal with the rationale behind service learning, its history, and its particular value for teaching sociology. I devote the second day of class to the concept of service learning. The students read a brief article by Andrea Roufs, "The History of Service-learning: A Synopsis of the Literature." Then I read aloud selected passages from Carla Howery's "Sociology, Service, and Learning, for a Stronger Discipline." This helps introduce students to both service learning and sociology. I also make an analogy between laboratory sections for physical science courses and service learning as the "lab" for the social sciences. This seems to make sense to the students and generates some enthusiasm for the activity.

A second strategy for addressing student resistance to service learning is the use of peer mentors. One of the expressions of student resistance to service learning is procrastination—students fail to do a service-learning activity or to start early enough to complete the required hours. Sometimes students simply have difficulty getting started. In addition, as previously noted, reflection activities are essential to integrating the service learning experience into the course, but with a large class size (typically thirty-five to forty students) it is often difficult for all students to have a chance to participate. With these issues in mind, I decided to try having peer mentors in the class.

I recruit three to five successful students from an earlier semester to serve as peer mentors for independent study credit. Peer mentors help integrate the service experience into the course and gain valuable experience in the process. They serve as role models, help students choose and begin a service-learning project, lead small group reflection sessions, and assist with other projects. It has been a great learning experience for them and also helps solve the problem of resistance while facilitating the integration of the service experiences into the classroom.

OUTCOMES

Overall, the course reviews have been very positive. Student outcomes indicate that the service learning component helps achieve course objectives. For example, according to student evaluation surveys, a large majority of students:

- agreed that the service-learning component enhanced their learning in the course.
- reported that the service-learning experience in the course made them more aware of community needs.

Many students wrote in journals and on student evaluation forms that they were inspired to continue their service work. Their comments include: "I plan on being more active in my community" and "I plan on keeping this up and getting others interested in it."

Although I sometimes encounter initial resistance to service learning, by the end of the semester students come to see the value of this approach to learning. In fact, many comment that it was their favorite part of the course and thank me for providing the opportunity to get involved.

One student made this comment on her final exam: "This class has changed my way of thinking on so many issues. You have really changed the way I look at things. . . . I come home from class each day and pass on what I have learned to family. . . . I hope to take what I have learned and maybe change things one little step at a time." I couldn't be more pleased.

I opened this chapter with Peter Berger's warning about the effects of studying sociology. I agree that learning about the nature of the world can be upsetting and, for some, even lead to feelings of hopelessness. However, it is my belief that studying sociology, especially with a service-learning component, can counteract hopelessness with feelings of efficacy. That is why I teach sociology and why I use service learning. As Virginia Gildersleeve (an early twentieth century educator) put it: "The ability to think straight, some knowledge of the past, some vision of the future, some skill to do useful service, some urge to fit that service into the well-being of the community...these are the most vital things education must try to produce."

References

Cooperative Institutional Research Program (CIRP). "2001 Freshmen Survey." *Higher Education Research Institute at UCLA,* 2001.

Eyler, Janet, and Dwight E. Giles, Jr. *Where's the Learning in Service Learning?* San Francisco: Jossey-Bass, 1999.

Eyler, Janet S., Dwight E. Giles, Jr., Christine M. Stenson, and Charlene J. Gray. "At a Glance: What We Know about the Effects of Service-Learning on College Students, Faculty, Institutions and Communities, 1993–2000." Learn and Serve America National Service Learning Clearinghouse, 2001. http://www.compact.org/resource/aag.pdf.

Hironimus-Wendt, Robert J., and Larry Lovell-Troy. "Grounding Service Learning in Social Theory." *Teaching Sociology* 27 (1999): 360–372.

Howery, Carla B. "Sociology, Service, and Learning, for a Stronger Discipline." Pp. 151–155 in *Cultivating the Sociological Imagination: Concepts and Models for Service-Learning in Sociology,* edited by James Ostrow, Garry Hesser, and Sandra Enos. Washington, DC: American Association for Higher Education, 1999.

Mills, C. Wright. *The Sociological Imagination.* New York: Grove Press, 1959.

Mooney, Linda A., and Bob Edwards. "Experiential Learning in Sociology: Service Learning and Other Community-Based Learning Initiatives." *Teaching Sociology* 29 no. 2 (2001): 181–194.

Myers-Lipton, Scott. "Effect of a Comprehensive Service-Learning Program on College Students' Civic Responsibility." *Teaching Sociology* 26 no. 4 (1998): 243–258.

Ostrow, James, Garry Hesser, and Sandra Enos, Eds. *Cultivating the Sociological Imagination: Concepts and Models for Service-Learning in Sociology.* Washington, DC: American Association for Higher Education, 1999.

Roufs, Andrea. "The History of Service Learning: A Synopsis of the Literature." *The Server (Learn and Serve America National Service Learning Clearinghouse Newsletter).* Summer 2000.

Sullivan-Catlin, Heather. "Food, Hunger, and Poverty: A Thematic Approach to Integrating Service-Learning." *Teaching Sociology* 30 no. 1 (2002): 39–52.

SUNY Potsdam. Spring 2000 SUNY Student Opinion Project. *Teaching Sociology* 26 no. 4 (1998).

3

Shaking the City's Walls: Teaching Politics with Bruce Springsteen

John Massaro
Department of Politics

> Individual freedom when it's not connected to some sort of community or friend or the world outside ends up feeling pretty meaningless.
> —Bruce Springsteen, Los Angeles Sports Arena, 1988

> I never realized until this [Springsteen] course how much of a fan Bruce is of fans.
> —SUNY Potsdam college student, January 2001

I teach a course, "Walk Tall: Political Themes in the Life and Lyrics of Bruce Springsteen," at SUNY Potsdam. Many people, including the SUNY Board of Trustees, apparently question whether there can be any possible links between Springsteen, rock 'n roll, and politics. Well, one well-respected Greek philosopher, a fellow named Plato, saw a very real connection between music and politics. He once observed that "when modes of music change, the fundamental laws of the state always change with them" (Plato, 113). More than 2,000 years later, another scholar of music, Jerry Lee Lewis, simply looked around the rock scene and concluded there was a "whole lot of shaken' going on." Taken in combination, Plato and Jerry Lee suggest that music has the capacity to shake the political system. Rock, rockers and, of course, Bruce Springsteen can be and, indeed, often are political.

19

One way in which Bruce Springsteen's music and all popular music can be political stems from a common failing in the way most of us listen—or actually don't listen—to lyrics in pop and especially rock. Most people, more than 60 percent, according to one estimate, listen to rock n' roll without paying any attention at all to the lyrics (Gracyk, 1996, 65). This enables any potential message manipulators to more easily interpret the lyrics of rock to support or otherwise reinforce their agenda. Manipulating messages, of course, forms a significant part of contemporary political life with its attention to propaganda, "spin," and sound bites.

Ronald Reagan, whether intentionally or not, was surely one of these people. He once said that the Springsteen song, "Born in the USA," conveyed a "message of hope." Of course, if Reagan ever really listened to the lyrics of "Born in the USA," he would have realized Springsteen is not at all focused on hope. On the contrary, Springsteen is indicting the United States for its alleged racist, imperialistic war against the Vietnamese and for the deplorable treatment of its returning Vietnam veterans. Note the following words that start the song: "Born down in a dead man's town, the first kick I took was when I hit the ground. You end up like a dog that been beat too much 'til you spend half your life just covering up." This is hardly the upbeat vision of hope and patriotism Reagan envisioned. Bruce also tells us that the Americans who fought and died in this war were not primarily, if at all, the children of the wealthy elite but rather the sons and daughters of the working class and the poor. The U.S. criminal justice system often cut a deal with these unfortunate souls by offering them a position in the military in place of a prison sentence. Springsteen conveys this by noting the vet in "Born in the USA," "got into a little hometown jam, so they put a rifle in my hand. Sent me off to a foreign land, to go and kill the yellow man." Also note that the returning vet can find neither personally or financially rewarding work in the United States even a decade after returning from the Vietnam War. Springsteen tells us in words that Reagan, and many others, never heard that the vet, who served his country well, now has "nowhere to run, ain't got nowhere to go."

Beyond my desire to make my students more aware of the politically relevant messages present in some rock lyrics, my reasons for offering the course range from the self-indulgent to the scholarly. I am a professor of politics and a Springsteen fan. Springsteen and I stand on some common ground. We were born and raised in New Jersey, share an Italian heritage (Bruce's mother's maiden name was Zirilli, my mother's was Cirelli), our fathers once worked as bus drivers, we both had severe and tortuous cases of acne as teenagers, and we spent many years "down" the shore "chasin' the factory girls under the boardwalk." Self-indulgence aside, a major justification for the course is that Springsteen's lyrics powerfully express how one's political consciousness develops—or, at least, can ideally develop.

The "Walk Tall" course highlights three significant themes: alienation, individualism, and love. Springsteen's writing about such themes can help in the crucial quest for self-understanding and political effectiveness. And because the course is offered primarily to young college students confronting identity concerns at one of life's critical crossroads, Springsteen's message can be especially meaningful and beneficial.

These three themes correspond to critical stages in human development (Erikson, 1982, 55–82, Nussbaum, 1997, 60, Primeaux, 1996, 1-15, passim). In the adolescent stage, humans are generally absorbed with discovering their individuality and in that daunting self-discovery process often experience alienation and confusion as well as indifference to concerns beyond themselves. Adolescents then advance to a young adulthood stage in which, as individuals, they attempt to make their own impact on the external world in many diverse ways, including, of course, through personal achievement. In the adult stage, well-adjusted individuals become capable of establishing genuinely loving and healthy relationships with an ever-widening circle of people. Despite the seemingly lockstep nature of these stages, people do not inevitably or easily pass through them like turnstiles at a subway station. Life is not so neat and tidy. Concerns about alienation, individuality, and love endure.

ADOLESCENCE: ALIENATION, LONELINESS, FEAR, AND CONFUSION

Springsteen's lyrics reflect the alienation, loneliness, fear, and confusion prominent in adolescence. The alienated teenager of "Growin' Up" not only strolls "all alone through a fallout zone" but when asked to "sit down," he must "stand up." The autobiographical "Bad Scooter" (Bruce Springsteen) of "Tenth Avenue Freeze Out" finds that while the "whole world's walking pretty," he's still "searching for his groove." Springsteen's young and lost people, insecure in their own identity, can be without a clue in trying to comprehend significant political forces shaping their environment and, like the souls of "Badlands," can get "caught in a cross fire that [they] don't understand."

Two of Springsteen's earlier and most famous songs, "Thunder Road" and "Born to Run," reflect in detail the themes associated with adolescence. The young and confused lover of "Thunder Road" pleads with his girlfriend, Mary, "not to turn him home again" because he "just cannot face [himself] alone again"—clear cry of alienation and loneliness. He also confesses his own fear about going out on the mysterious and unknown highway of life, Thunder Road, seeing it as "lying out there like a killer in the sun," not unlike a rattlesnake in the afternoon heat waiting to attack youthful, inexperienced prey such as Bruce and Mary.

In class discussions, I particularly stress the gender equality in the lyrics of "Thunder Road." This equality suggests that the themes of alienation, loneliness, fear, and confusion are universal human concerns shared by both genders in their adolescent years, if not throughout their lives. For example, Springsteen notes that Mary is not a striking, drop-dead gorgeous Cameron Diaz-type. She is just a regular everyday, common young woman who, as Springsteen tells us, "ain't a beauty" but she's "alright." But Springsteen notes that while Mary is nothing special, neither is he, describing himself as "not a hero" and as one who can only offer Mary the redemption that lies "beneath his dirty hood." Equality of the sexes is also seen in Springsteen's promise that he will not be Mary's knight in shining armor nor will he put her on a pedestal like some fragile doll. Their relationship is one approaching equality. He tells her: "My car's out back if you're ready to make that long, long walk from your front porch to my front seat. The door's open but the ride it ain't free."

I also highlight "Thunder Road's" classic last line, signaling the way many alienated young people feel about the confines and restrictions of the towns in which they were raised. While many of us come to love our hometown as we age, as adolescents, we are bound to see it the way the main character of "Thunder Road" does: "It's a town full of losers and I'm pullin' out of here to win."

"Born to Run," of course, is another Springsteen anthem for all those lost, confused, and scared young people. Springsteen suggests that these troubled adolescents might often feel that fleeing from their responsibilities and embracing the escape promised by a car and the open road remain their only hope of deliverance and salvation. Note the lyrics of a typical but fitting teenage drama and exaggeration in "Born to Run": "Baby this town rips the bones from your back. It's a death trap. It's a suicide rap. We gotta get out while we're young cause tramps like us, baby, we were born to run." Notice also that these runners just want to run. They really have no idea where they are going. There is no mature plan beyond flight.

Because the students perceived their very own feelings about adolescence articulated by Springsteen, a common bond soon connected them. (Please note that all references to student responses to Springsteen's lyrics are taken from course journals, without the writer being identified for reasons of privacy.) One student attributed this connection to her finding that Springsteen's lyrics can "often parallel meanings in each of our lives." Assessing the lyrics of Springsteen's "Wild Billy's Circus Story," another student took some comfort in the fact that "like the individuals of the circus, Springsteen often felt like an outsider, mainly when he was younger." Another seemingly, if momentarily, alienated class participant confided, "I want to be Mary and jump in his [Bruce's] car and ride off down Thunder Road. Who knows what lies ahead, but it can't get much worse or disappointing." Another student acquainted with the struggles of adolescence succinctly noted the fear and confusion she was confronting at this stage in her life: "I am at the point where I have to choose where to drive; so "Thunder Road" is a relevant song. There is a large level of uncertainty when you are in your early twenties, and this is accompanied by fear."

Young Adulthood: Individualism and Fighting Back

In a second stage of psychological/political development, adolescents begin advancing to a young adulthood level where, as individuals, they begin to find themselves and to make their own impact on the external world. Springsteen's lyrics emphasize this theme of individuality, especially in the form of self-assertion. The troubled young man of "Growin Up" glimpses a ray of hope in his ability to find "the key to the universe in the engine of an old parked car." In "New York City Serenade," Springsteen advises that those who can "walk tall" will best traverse the mean streets of life. In this context, to "walk tall" signifies the self-assertion of either actually being proud and unafraid or at least trying to appear that way. Asserting individuality through achievement is evident in "Thunder Road" as the young man expresses personal pride in learning "how to make it [his guitar] talk." The empowerment associated with finding one's individuality is reflected in the once alienated Bad Scooter now confidently able to "bust this city in half."

Developing one's individualism, one's unique talents and abilities, is politically significant because it emboldens people to fight to shape the world to reflect their own hopes and dreams. This phenomenon is vividly portrayed in Springsteen's "Badlands," "Racing in the Street," and "Darkness on the Edge of Town."

In "Badlands," the escapist running away of "Thunder Road" and "Born to Run" end and Springsteen's maturing protagonist no longer meekly succumbs to or flees from life's troubles but stands and fights back against perceived evils. Rather than fleeing these troubles, he or she now wants to defiantly "spit in the face of these Badlands." As Springsteen states: "Badlands you gotta live it everyday. Let the broken hearts stand for the price you've gotta pay. We'll keep pushin' till it's understood and these Badlands start treating us good." I also stress the fact that in "Badlands," Springsteen begins conveying a more generalized, if oversimplified, version of the nature of politics in the United States: "Poor man wanna be rich. Rich man wanna be king. And a king ain't satisfied til he rules everything."

In "Racin' in the Streets," Springsteen tells us that people who never learn to follow their own individualistic spirit will likely be devoured by life. These poor souls will, according to Springsteen, "start dying little by little, piece by piece." On the other hand, those maturing individuals with a well-developed sense of self will be able to withstand even the backbreaking and dispiriting work they might be forced to endure in the competitive and unforgiving U.S. political/economic system. Their individualistic passion, in Springsteen's metaphoric words, will enable them to "come home from work, wash up, and go racin' in the street." And he offers a universal call to youth to not immaturely run away or passively accept their plight in life, but to fight back against system-imposed limitations. There clearly is political meaning, if not an outright defiant warning, in "Racin's" final stanza: "Tonight, tonight, the highway's bright. Out of my way, Mister, you better keep. 'Cause Summer's here and the time is right. We're going racin' in the street."

And finally, the determination to fight back is clearly seen in the protagonist of "Darkness on the Edge of Town." Springsteen suggests that even for those who try to run away from life, from their roots, there will always be a reckoning with the pain and sorrow of life we can never escape. He metaphorically describes this reckoning as the "darkness on the edge of town." And what do you do when you confront that inevitable darkness? Immature, insufficiently politically developed people try to escape from responsibility by flight or avoidance or even death, but not so the mature, politically conscious individual. He or she goes out to confront the danger directly. As Springsteen notes:

> Tonight I'll be on that hill 'cause I can't stop
> I'll be on that hill with everything I got.
> Lives on the line where dreams are found and lost.
> I'll be there on time and I'll pay the cost
> For wanting things that can only be found
> In the darkness on the edge of town.

Students in the class clearly saw their own quest for individualism and self-actualization reflected in Springsteen's lyrics. One noted in her journal: "You have to make yourself happy. You have to love yourself and fight for yourself. Your work or partner can add happiness but in the end it's just you and so you better like who you are." Similarly, another student, employing Springsteen's favorite metaphors, wrote: "This is the point where I am supposed to figure out how to make my guitar talk. There are many roads I can take. I think the point is I at least have to try one road, rather than stay stagnant."

ADULTHOOD: EXPANDING CIRCLES OF LOVE

In the third stage of mature or adult political/psychological development, well-adjusted individuals become capable of looking, and loving, beyond themselves. They can begin to establish genuinely loving relationships with an ever-widening circle of people and communities. Beyond the most important love of self, the theme of mature love appears in Springsteen's lyrics in at least four related forms. These involve love of a partner, friends, children, and community.

The first of these, romantic love, is a common and prevalent theme in popular music and Springsteen has written his fair share of these songs. One of my favorites in this genre is Springsteen's "If I Should Fall Behind." In this song, Springsteen openly pledges his mature commitment to stay by his partner's, his soul mate's, side throughout their life together, no matter what troubles befall them. His pledge is simple but profound: "I will wait for you and should I fall behind, wait for me." The song represents the beauty reflected in the intimate and unqualified love between a couple. And yet this song becomes even more poignant and powerful when, in performance, Springsteen and The E Street Band, including Bruce's spouse, Patti Scialfa, turn it into not simply a celebration of the love between a man and a woman but of the love that can also exist among good friends.

Springsteen's lyrics of love, romance, and friendship reflect his belief that in a genuine loving relationship, all lovers gain in a strength that is so much greater than the sum of their parts. This is Bruce's way of suggesting that it is the inherent power of love of a partner or friends that enable the lovers and friends to conquer forces together that would easily defeat them as separate individuals. Such empowerment is, of course, interpersonal and political.

Today, Springsteen is a father with three children. He quite maturely recognizes not only the wonderful joy of loving and being loved by a child but also the potential for sorrow and vulnerability that comes with that love. Mature people understand that they cannot truly love another without opening themselves to the risks of loss and pain. And both the love and potential for loss and pain intensify even more with a parent's love of a child. Springsteen wrote the song "Living Proof" immediately after the birth of his first son. Its lyrics resonate with all parents and parents-to-be when thinking of their children. Note particularly the spiritual power Springsteen identifies as a parent views his or her child for the first time. As Springsteen puts it: "In his mother's arms, it was all the beauty I could take like the missing words to some prayer that I could never make." Also notice how this weak, vulnerable, needy infant has the contradictory capacity to instill his or her parents with strength, understanding, redemption, and power (politics again) they had lost or perhaps never had. Speaking directly to his infant son, Springsteen notes:

> You shot through my anger and rage
> To show me my prison was just an open cage
> There were no keys, no guards
> Just one frightened man and some old shadows for bars.

And notice how Springsteen, aware of the vulnerability of love and the fragility of all life, reminds us (and himself) never to shrink from love and its inevitable responsibilities. Rather, he asks all to fiercely and passionately embrace them in the short and precious time lovers have together.

> Life is just a house of cards
> As fragile as each and every breath
> Of this boy sleepin' in our bed.
> Tonight, let's lie beneath the eaves
> Just a close band of happy thieves.
> And when that train comes we'll get on board
> And steal what we can from the treasures, the treasures of the
>   Lord.
> It's been a long, long drought, baby.
> Tonight the rain's pouring down on our roof.
> Looking for a little of God's mercy,
> I found living proof.

More recently, Springsteen's lyrics speak of that most mature stage of political development when a person becomes concerned not only with self and immediate family but also with his or her community and the larger world beyond. In "The Ghost of Tom Joad," Springsteen signals his willingness to fight on behalf of the oppressed, noting, as did Tom Joad in *The Grapes of Wrath*, "Wherever somebody's strugglin' to be free, look in their eyes, Mom, you'll see me." In the song, "Youngstown," Springsteen speaks through the voice of an exploited steelworker deserted by all those he made "rich enough to forget my name." He reminds us in ironic and political terms that in shutting down Youngstown's steel plants, the "big boys, the owners, did what Hitler couldn't do."

Springsteen also presents a dramatic illustration of the victory of communal love over ethnic hatred in the beautiful "Galveston Bay." A combination of racial and economic politics push a Gulf shrimper, an American Vietnam veteran, to a seemingly inevitable act of violence against a former military ally, a Vietnamese Vietnam veteran. As the moment of deadly confrontation approaches, the American vet compassionately opts for tolerance over revenge and for a communal casting of both American and Vietnamese nets into the lifegiving waters of Galveston Bay.

In "American Skin (41 Shots)," Springsteen draws upon the New York City police's controversial and allegedly racially tinged slaying of Amadou Diallo. He conveys, among other political concerns, a pragmatic warning to young minorities that they should "always be polite" to police authorities or run the risk of being "killed just for living in your American skin."

Finally, Springsteen's love of community, the most mature political act, is reflected in "Land of Hope and Dreams." In this song, the struggle for equality for all people is epitomized in a simple train heading to a destination of sunshine and freedom and taking on all people, not only saints, winners, and kings, but also the more numerous of us, sinners, losers, whores, gamblers, fools, and the broken-hearted.

The students responded knowingly to Springsteen's communal themes. One wrote: "I realize how fortunate I am to have been born into a middle class family. I don't deserve the hand I've been dealt anymore than the people in his [Springsteen's] stories deserve the hand they have been dealt. I could have just as easily been sleeping beneath an underpass or trying to sneak across the border."

Another student avowed that she learned from listening to Springsteen that "just not being racist is not enough. We have to fight for equality because that's what we would want if we were in the minority and because it's right." Another student praised Springsteen for forcing us to take a hard look "at the often-hyped 'Forrest Gumpness' of the USA vs. the Youngtowns." And finally, one student, astutely noting a more universal theme in "American Skin" beyond its controversial focus on one New York City tragedy, concluded that the community of which Springsteen sings is "one where every life is valuable. The bloody river isn't just for the officer praying in the vestibule, it is for all of us, because if we live in a community saturated by hatred and do nothing, then we too are stained."

The night, in 1988, when Bruce uttered the epigram about individual freedom that heads this chapter, he also remarked that it's all about "looking for connections and I guess that's why I am here tonight." Millions of my generation, Springsteen's contemporaries, know he has connected with them. The thoughtful responses of the students in my course convey a hopeful promise that Springsteen will continue to make connections with today's and future generations. In so doing, their lives—and communities—will be enriched.

REFERENCES

Erikson, Erik H. *The Life Cycle Completed: A Review*. New York: Norton, 1982.

Gracyk, Theodore. *Rhythm and Noise: An Aesthetics of Rock*. Durham, NC: Duke University Press, 1996.

Nussbaum, Martha C. *Cultivating Humanity: A Classical Defense of Reform in Liberal Education*. Cambridge: Harvard University Press, 1997.

Plato. *The Republic. The Dialogues of Plato, Vol. III*, translated by B. Jowett, 3rd ed. New York: Macmillan, 1892.

Primeaux, Pat. *The Moral Passion of Bruce Springsteen*. San Francisco: International Scholars, 1996.

4

Border Crossing in the North Country: An Academic Story

Liliana Trevizán
Department of Modern Languages

> *Un mundo que demandaría a mi madre, como demanda a todos los hijos de immigrantes, que abandonara la lengua de sus ancestros, el precio que tenía que pagar si quería ir pasando por esa puerta.*
> —Ariel Dorfman

Crossing disciplinary boundaries in academia may be as challenging and adventurous—and even as dangerous at times—as crossing national borders or traveling through continents. Based on my own teaching experience at SUNY Potsdam, I suggest that the experience is also as rewarding and inspirational as world traveling.

At the start of the spring 2001 semester I had no idea I would enjoy one of the most rewarding experiences in ten years of teaching. My four classes included two sections of Spanish 103 and the senior Spanish 462 seminar I had developed, entitled Border Crossing/ Cruzar fronteras. In addition, I was to teach Approaches to Women's Studies (WMST 100), the introductory course of the Women's Studies Program. Due to course content, I often cross-list my Spanish seminars with Women's Studies (WS) and I occasionally also teach a Literature in Translation course that is WS designated.

Creating the Border Crossing seminar was exciting because it allowed me to bring Latin American and Latino literatures together. Until that spring, I had not had the opportunity to explore this intersection in my teaching, even though I had already explored it in my writing and publications. At an undergraduate institution, modern language faculty switch roles constantly—one hour they become skillful instructors for the teaching of the second language and the next they change gears to teach literature, culture, and film. At times this role switching can be distressing and sometimes more than a bit schizophrenic. Even though college teachers may welcome a challenging multitasking workday, perhaps they all experience something of a psychological split between the teaching of lower and upper division classes. Personally, I believe this split greatly affects language teachers even more, especially instructors of French, Spanish, German, or any other second language.

For me, the most gratifying aspect of the 2001 spring semester was to see my teaching reflecting my whole professional persona. Teaching the Border Crossing/Cruzar fronteras and Approaches to Women's Studies courses the same semester allowed me to see the many ways in which different courses can cross-pollinate one another and also stimulate new scholarship. This experience was an extraordinary learning opportunity for both my students and myself. By the end of the semester, I was convinced that the fluid relationship between the two classes I was teaching had become a terrific pedagogical tool I should attempt to undertake and benefit from more often.

One important aspect of these two classes was their composition, since more than by syllabi or class preparation, teaching is always shaped by the individual students who take a given class. Like many small state schools, SUNY Potsdam has a very homogenous student body, mostly composed of first-generation students, whose education stems, more often than not, from a regimented curriculum established by the State of New York.

My WS 100 course caused me some anxiety at first. I wondered if students were going to take my class to "only" receive a grade and four credits and meet none of the always precious General Education components.[1] On the first day of class I was pleasantly surprised: I had twenty-nine enrolled students, and two were male. The class had an almost even distribution of sophomores and first-year students, as well as a few seniors; they were in a variety of majors, ranging from Anthropology and Business, to English, Psychology, and Biology. Only two were minority students, and perhaps one-third of the class had taken other Women's Studies classes before. Two students had already declared the WS minor. I knew three of them from previous classes and one student was a Spanish major.

My Border Crossing seminar enrolled eighteen, which is unusually high for seminars. It made me quite proud that out of the eighteen, fifteen were Spanish majors, including all of the graduating seniors for that year. Two seniors in other departments, who were fluent in Spanish, also took the class because they were intrigued by its description. One high school teacher was taking the class for credit toward her master's degree. Seven of the students were male, six were Hispanic, and two were African American. I had seven "nontraditional" students in my seminar who were in their late twenties or early thirties, working full-time, and some of them parenting. Eleven students were living in the campus dorms.

My syllabus for Border Crossing included three lengthy books. The first one was Isabel Allende's 400-page fascinating novel in Spanish, *Daughter of Fortune* (2000). Beautifully written, the novel tells the adventurous story of a woman of obscure lineage, born in Chile at the turn of the century, who travels to California following the Gold Rush. After numerous adventures and much growing up, she succeeds in making a good living for herself, while also finding a loving partner in a Chinese man who practices alternative medicine. The second text in my syllabus was a 300-page memoir, *Heading South, Looking North* (1998) by Latin Americanist scholar and Duke professor Ariel Dorfman. Also a story of displacement and travel, this memoir is really a metaphor to describe our intense investment in a given identity, and how much exile and immigration resemble the experiences people go through when they see themselves affected by sudden changes and displacement. As an exploration of the power of language, the book offers a sophisticated reading of a Jew's experience in South and North America within the historical frame of the cold war. Dorfman would enchant my students by his certainty that "one cannot grow unless one breaks out and learns and opens up to what is strange and foreign and fertile" (Dorfman, 1998, 276).

The last book of literature in my syllabus was *Making Faces/Haciendo Caras* (1988), edited by Gloria Anzaldúa. This is a 400-page collection of writings by Chicana and Latina women authors, featuring essays, criticism, short stories, and poetry. These are powerful pieces inscribing women within the immigration process, or the experience of living between the national narratives of the United States and Mexico, or in the intersection between both. To introduce a more complex reading of what it means to be an American today, the latter were, in sum, a multiplicity of sophisticated women's texts shot through with class and social differences as well as lesbian discourses. The fourth item that occupied our seminar was the British film *Tango Lesson* (1998) by Sally Potter, a splendid artistic piece filmed mostly in black and white, with a few scenes in Technicolor, whose story unfolds in Paris, Quebec, and Buenos Aires. Through dance and light and shadow explorations, Potter conveys North/South power relations as they are imprinted on exiled, displaced individuals. A love story told simultaneously in Spanish, English, and French, this film is also a poignant, seductive tango of exile, dislocation, and new forged identities. Our last piece to study was the film *All about My Mother* (1999), by Academy Award winner and Spanish film director Pedro Almodóvar. A bold, farcical, and hilarious piece, this is also a truly witty movie that deconstructs gender, race, and ethnicity. Almodóvar's rhetoric links motherhood to AIDS in a dazzling film that earned the director his second Oscar for Best Foreign Film. Forced to be in the margins of citizenry and living among prostitutes, transvestites, and the homeless, Argentine revolutionaries exiled in Spain since the seventies experience this superb and compassionate story of survival in which the fluctuating identities of a number of drama queens are affected by death, abandonment, and pain, but also by profound love and hope. In total, my students were required to read more than 1,200 pages of literature, view two films, read ten articles, write five papers, keep a reading journal, and also watch other films on their own.[2]

I was happy with my syllabus; I had selected wonderful contemporary pieces that showed the meaningful imprints of the experience of border crossing on the human experience. All these texts presented our class with a repertoire of life situations in which individuals, despite having being stripped at one time or another of their comforting identity narratives, courageously confront multiple demons with a true sense of wholeness.

Considering my teaching of both the Spanish seminar and the Introduction to Women's Studies course, soon after the semester began I started wondering how much of a "border crossing" I myself was experiencing. Ever concerned about minimizing the effect that my Spanish accent could have on students, I had perhaps overlooked the fact that students had known my work as WS director for five years and had great expectations from the class. Furthermore, generous and open-minded from the very beginning, they honestly thought that my background was a valuable source of knowledge for the class. If my students' committed attitudes were intriguing to me, they were also truly rewarding.

As a full-time Modern Languages faculty at SUNY Potsdam, I dedicate 50 percent of my teaching load to lower division language classes. I love my students of Spanish 101, 102, and 103. The fact that I always have waiting lists in every single class might be due to the fact that we do not offer enough sections of a required course, but it may also be a sign that students find my teaching effective. I earned my Ph.D. in Romance Language Literature with a specialization in Contemporary Latin American narrative and wrote a dissertation on the politics of sexuality in Latin American women's writing. Because of my academic background, I felt very well prepared for teaching the Women's Studies course. Nevertheless, the course presented me with one particular challenge: how to give to my students an appealing selection of concepts, authors, and issues so as to not overwhelm them with scholarship and information. The experience of professional freedom that teaching outside departmental boundaries allows faculty was indeed new to me. Was I myself literally crossing a border every time I went from one to the other side of the building to teach WS 101? I did not mention it to my students, but the tremendous amount of preparation the course demanded was absolutely compensated for by the sense that this work was completely my own responsibility.

The exhilarating feeling of anticipation that freedom offers to those who risk the unknown is a literary topic in the travel literature we explored endlessly in our Border Crossing seminar when we followed characters such as Eliza, the protagonist of Isabel Allende's novel. As a young woman, she travels from Valparaiso to San Francisco to join the thousands attracted by the Gold Rush fever and "in the process, she manages to transform the emphasis of a well known story belonging to North American lore and introduces the foreign as a significant force in the U.S. West" (Masiello, 2001, 132).

After two weeks, I used the fishbowl technique in a segment of every Women's Studies class session: a pair of students would present on articles they had prepared, and others would then take turns sitting on an extra chair in the middle of a circle to voice their opinion. After that preparation, my students participated regularly in class discussions. I encouraged critical thinking through a class discussion setting modeled after a democratic forum. At the beginning of the course, we agreed to follow certain guidelines: talk on the topic, listen to each other, disagree respectfully, avoid interruptions, and allow any student to pass on the discussion once. Responses in reading journals helped students to gradually prepare for their presentations and their final papers. In their journals, I asked them to write at least three arguments against and one in favor of each assigned article, and to collect quotations for their final papers. In order to help them add complexity to their original writing, every week I gave them back their journals with my comments and questions.

With care and respect, controversial issues such as race, abortion, lesbianism, rape, and incest were discussed early on in my course. Surprisingly, mother–daughter relationship issues, pay equity, beauty, and breast cancer were much more emotionally engaging and even distressing topics to discuss for some of my students than topics that at first seemed would easily trigger a lot of discussion. The inclusion of my students' experiences facilitated intellectual connections between their personal narratives and history. However, it was not always easy to resist the temptation to generalize so that the class had to keep reminding itself, "the moment that one assumes that one knows what female experience is, one runs the risk of creating another reductive operation" (Johnson, 1987, 46). Small-group work, in-class sharing of individual writing, peer review, debate, and other diverse strategies of teaching and learning made the class lively and, above all, forced students to be prepared and to carefully read the assigned texts for each class. This, in turn, allowed my lectures to be synthetic and explore the issues at a level of sophistication unusual for an introductory level class. I must admit that at first I was somewhat uncomfortable thinking that perhaps I was pressing students into too much reading. On the other hand, I felt compelled to cover what colleagues who regularly teach this class were covering, using a textbook that, if mostly centered in the American experience, was an excellent textbook to teach WS 100.[3] I understood that my responsibility was to cover what my colleagues would in that course, and I did so. Many extra readings on my own, much class preparation, and above all a strong feminist theoretical background helped me with the task. We reviewed basic concepts, explored issues, analyzed texts, learned facts, and criticized theories.

I also felt compelled to teach what I know best, Third World feminism. I had selected a wonderful textbook centered on women's human rights, with articles mostly written by Third World feminists.[4] I did not want to relegate these texts to being just appendices to the class. I would have been doing a clear disservice to my students had I not provided them with the best information at hand. Thus, in the third week of classes, once they were comfortable with my teaching style, I assigned one article from the human rights text. The result was mindblowing. My students' response was so enthusiastic that I realized they were genuine with their questions and, instead of waiting to finish one text to advance to the next, we decided to equally divide our reading assignments between the two textbooks. It was a timely decision that allowed students to make unsuspected connections and widen the scope of their expectations. For instance, while we were reading the classic "Judging the Beauty Judges" by Gloria Steinem, we also read a text, "Liberation Day" by Christa Wolf, that describes the effect war has on a girl growing up during the Nazi occupation. Reading Luisa Valenzuela's stories on censorship in Latin America brought another layer of complexity to our conversation on civil liberties. The fact is that several of our discussions on readings on human rights and poverty yielded to a critical conversation that would have not sprung up easily from more traditional readings. And to make theory the stuff of daily life, one group assignment required students to visit a local department store, such as Walmart, and focus on a telling aspect that elucidated the interplay of gender differences at work in everyday life. Many groups, as expected, concentrated their analysis on the toys aisle, with the boy/blue versus girl/pink distinction, and dolls versus Legos, or the like. Interestingly enough, however, some of the groups also considered the global implications of the politics of gender on the local market. This came as a surprise to me because students had been very critical of the lecture on globalization by Chandra Talpade Mohanty we had attended at Saint Lawrence University the week before I gave this assignment.[5] But her lecture had evidently influenced their presentations. When they attended Cornell professor Debra Castillo's lecture on the politics of the U.S./Mexico border later on in the semester, they engaged from the very beginning in the discussion and asked Dr. Castillo several pointed questions.[6]

In the Border Crossing seminar, all students contributed greatly to the critical emphasis of our readings and it was evident that the best conversations occurred when students were assigned to debate from a position different from their own. Since a most effective teaching tool in my seminar sessions is to give students authority, I start the class letting students around the table speak and focus on a fragment they want us to cover that day. In general, the strategies of participation I devised for my seminar that spring semester were successful in that they took students from an initial observation to a more sophisticated level of literary analysis to making unsuspected connections. I made sure this process took place according to relevant sources by always requiring them to contribute an actual quote or textual evidence to back up their comments. The responses of the students throughout the semester as well as their written evaluations of the class were immensely positive. Clearly aware that "students' judgments of what happens in a classroom are a function not only of what material an instructor presents and how that presentation is accomplished but also of the authority students are willing to accord the instructor as a legitimate purveyor of scholarship and knowledge" (Lewis, 1999, 77), I take with a grain of salt the fact that a high percentage of students stated in their evaluations that mine had been one of the most meaningful courses they had ever taken during their college years. On the other hand, finding out that several of these students later on went on to receive academic awards at the Honors Convocation ceremony at the college was certainly gratifying.

The student evaluations for my course suggest that student contribution increases once one makes sure that all those involved in the process are equally valued and, I will claim here, when students know that the individual viewpoint they bring to the conversation is clearly appreciated. My students were appreciative of the level of reflection expected and they recognized that the course confronted them with intellectual challenges they had not encountered before. My teaching was also invigorated by the joy of confronting new challenges again.

To better present all the factors involved in my successful teaching experience during the spring semester of 2001, I need to place this experience within its institutional frame: first, because it may be useful to observe the creative work institutions promote today when allowing departmental structures to be instrumental in testing disciplinary boundaries and allowing faculty to move into newer fields of inquiry within the humanities and the study of culture; second, because this move makes it possible to produce and articulate the most wonderful teaching and some remarkable learning experiences from unexpected angles.

Normally we are led to believe that the institutional setting determines all the teaching we do and that is relatively true. Careful preparation, dedication, and scholarship can all in fact collude to create a perfect learning environment, but, as I learned from the same story, much of it also seems to happen as if by chance, if we embrace the opportunities presented to us, if we let the magic flow, no matter how far away they may seem to be carrying us at first.

My fifteen years of teaching at SUNY Potsdam have taught me that we are able to generate meaningful learning experiences when faculty engage in interdisciplinary teaching. This volume attests to some extraordinary pedagogical achievements that have resulted from the encouragement of interdisciplinary explorations. As a decisive contributing partner to such enterprises, the Women's Studies Program has also been shaped by it, configuring itself in the last ten years as a space where cross-disciplinary conversations are welcomed and fostered and where faculty from diverse backgrounds can make meaningful contributions. Indeed, our Women's Studies Program is one of the richest interdisciplinary pedagogical experiences the college has to offer. As of now, several academic departments of the College have benefited from supporting their faculty's explorations of interdisciplinary teaching.[7]

One of our most effective recruitment tools for attracting students already familiar with the more than thirty-year-old discourse of inclusion and diversity is to diversify the curriculum. Incorporating new approaches into disciplines and participating in interdisciplinary programs is precisely what Professor Nelly Furman has in mind in advising that a French program should address the need to create courses "attractive to students with pluridisciplinary interests, across national borders and historical time zones, answering the needs of today's society" (Furman, 1998, 79). Furthermore, the education that our students require in the twenty-first century is one that will help them solve problems created by the intermingling of different perspectives and different practices in a global marketplace. To seek and analyze systems, patterns, and interconnections can help solve those problems before they become irremediable. "But this kind of comprehensive pattern-seeking analysis is precisely what our current fragmentation of knowledge into disciplines and departments works against. Larger trends and patterns, however compelling, tend to be ignored within a discipline-centric context."[8]

Finally, I must prevent the reader from assuming that my experience led me to a road without any bumps. Even though it was indeed special, in the long run I will probably remember that semester as a blissful yet exhausting teaching experience. While teaching the Women's Studies introductory course, I realized that lower division courses are a different species, and that some aspects of teaching lower division courses I had attributed to my teaching of a 'foreign' language were in effect elements of teaching classes composed mostly of freshmen and sophomores. Thus, high levels of academic expectation, a need to engage in laborious work to always stay on track, an unbelievable trust of the instructor, along with the precious sense of wonder that students provide us when they start to understand something new, were all playing the same key role as in my Spanish lower division classes. That some days my Women's Studies students could not—or did not want to—engage on issues as personal as domestic violence, eating disorders, or pay equity was a surprise for me at the time, but now it is refreshing to come across the realization that Women's Studies teaching is as typical a teaching setting as any other—time and again instructors and students will go through a number of subtle and not so subtle negotiations so that effective teaching/learning takes place.

According to Herbert Lindenberger in his article "Breaking Boundaries, Making Connections," "Challenging traditional disciplinary and generic borders above all enables us to establish new connections and, one hopes, to encourage supportive institutional arrangements within our profession" (1998, 9). During periods of budget constraints, when resources are scarce, innovation may seem a luxury. In our institution, we know that the current economic reality of the State of New York will influence fiscal policy as well as politics. Contrary to what some may think, I believe this is precisely a timely moment to encourage cultural border crossing and disciplinary cross-pollination because interdisciplinary teaching will help us maximize the use of faculty expertise under difficult conditions. Also, incoming faculty will be a most remarkable asset for this purpose. Since they entered graduate school after interdisciplinary programs were well established, they are likely to have graduated with a strong interdisciplinary background and to have written a dissertation that tested the boundaries of their own disciplines. By encouraging these faculty to continue and expand on their own intellectual journey, we will be better serving our undergraduate population and, at the same time, energizing ourselves with many riveting learning opportunities for our students.[9]

NOTES

1. Under our General Education program, students take courses with a number of different designators to complete their Liberal Arts requirements. For example, Spanish 103 satisfies the Modern Language (ML) requirement.

2. They watched on their own *Women in Chile* (BBC/PBS, The Americas, 1992); *Making Sense of the Sixties* (USA/PBS, 1995); *Paris Is Burning* (New York, 1990); *Priscilla: Queen of the Dessert* (Australia, 1991), *Ma Vie en Rose* (France, 1990), and *Billy Eliot* (France, 1999).

3. See Susan Frank Ballentine and Jessica Barksdale Inclán, eds., *Diverse Voices of Woman*, Mayfield, 1995.

4. See Marjorie Agosin, *A Map of Hope: Women's Writing on Human Rights*, Rutgers University Press, 1998.

5. "Globalization and Multiculturalism" by Chandra Talpade Mohanty, February 2001. Mohanty is the editor of *Third World Feminism*, Duke University Press, 1990.

6. "Border Crossing: Mexico/USA" by Debra Castillo, SUNY Potsdam, March 10, 2001. Castillo is the author of *Talking Back: Toward a Latin American Feminist Literary Criticism*, Cornell University Press, 1992.

7. The Adirondack Cluster is one of the most sustained examples, but there are many others, such as the Africana Studies program, the Business of Music program, the Environmental Studies program, and the Native American Studies program. The departments of Anthropology and Sociology, among others, have benefited from the support they have rendered to those initiatives.

8. See Kolodny (2000), 136.

9. I am grateful to Anne Malone and Caroline Downing for their comments and editorial help.

REFERENCES

Dorfman, Ariel. *Heading South, Looking North*. New York: Farrar, Straus and Giroux, 1998.
Furman, Nelly. "French Studies: Back to the Future." *Profession* MLA (1998): 68–80.
Johnson, Barbara. *A World of Difference*. Baltimore: John Hopkins University Press, 1987.
Kolodny, Annette. "Women in Higher Education in the Twenty-first Century: Some Feminists and Global Perspectives." *NWSA Journal* 12 no. 2 (2000): 130–147.
Lewis, Magda. *The Backlash Factor, Everyday Knowledge and Uncommon Truths: Women of the Academy*, Linda Christian-Smith and Kristine Kellor, eds. Boulder: Westview, 1999.
Lindenberger, Herbert. "Breaking Boundaries, Making Connections." *Profession* MLA (1998): 4–10.
Luebke, B., and M. E. Reilly, Eds. *Women's Studies Graduates: The First Generation*. New York: Teachers College, 1995.
Masiello, Francine. *The Art of Transition: Latin American Culture and Neoliberal Crisis*. Durham, NC: Duke University Press, 2001.

5

Group Projects in Computer Science

Peter S. Brouwer
Computer Science

Computer science is not a discipline typically associated with innovative or progressive pedagogy. Its difficult content, rigorous mathematical foundations, and step-wise curriculum that insists on coverage at each level before moving to the next, discourage much in the way of experimental teaching. That many computer science graduates end up in industry with the promise of high salaries encourages a competitive learning environment for high grades and a desire for perceived relevance in knowledge and skills. Students want to know when and how course material will be applied in their budding careers. In addition, the archetype of the solo programmer "hacking" away late into the night gives the impression of the field as a solitary learning discipline. While there are some innovative pedagogical techniques espoused in the computer science education literature (e.g., closed labs, virtual development environments, simulations, etc.), for the most part, much of computer science pedagogy can be described as fairly traditional or conventional.

However, one thing that can surely be said about computer science coursework is that it provides multiple opportunities for active student learning. Typically, about half of the courses in a computer science degree program are what are commonly referred to as "programming courses." These are courses in which a significant component of the class activity is the learning of a programming language and/or the developing of program solutions to posed problems. To be successful in programming projects, a student must understand the problem at hand, design a solution, implement it in a programming language, and then test and debug the program. Put quite simply, students must do to learn. Clearly, the programming experience is a very active process that engages the student in a number of complex cognitive tasks. For instance, I have studied the wide variety of heuristic strategies that students use in the task of debugging their computer programs (Brouwer, 1993). There are also affective factors that are rarely considered—the discipline and perseverance to see a multistage project through to completion, the ability to cope with frustration and overcome obstacles, and the ability to work with others in a constructive manner with sensitivity to group dynamics. These affective factors are rarely addressed explicitly in any meaningful way by classroom instruction.

This chapter describes a large-scale, semester-long, team programming project that I have used with success. The objectives of this project activity go beyond the accumulation of content knowledge— although that is certainly an expected outcome. Students are also placed in a situation where, in order to be successful, they must organize a large task and break it down into component parts (project management), solve significant problems, interact successfully with a team of peers, and develop strong interpersonal communication skills.

Diana Oblinger (1999) has written about the skills students will have to develop to be competitive in the fast-changing world of the twenty-first century business environment. This constantly evolving high-technology business environment has led to the development of flexible organizations that require employees to be adaptive (they can change, learn new skills, and add to their knowledge) and transformative (they can see changes that need to be made and are able to work with people and the organization to transform the enterprise). Oblinger argues that several basic competencies that go beyond disciplinary knowledge will make employees valuable in flexible organizations and will afford career security:

- *Problem Solving*—This includes problem recognition, problem definition, formulating a problem-solving strategy, representing information, allocating resources, and monitoring and evaluating the solution.
- *Teamwork*—The increasing complexity of our world demands a team of people working together, each with a unique set of skills. A successful team requires discipline and strong interpersonal skills.
- *Interpersonal Skills*—These skills extend beyond writing, speaking, and listening to providing feedback, giving encouragement, delegating responsibility, and sharing recognition.

- *Creativity*—This is associated with being able to define and redefine problems in different ways, being able to analyze and evaluate ideas, and being able to deal with ambiguity.
- *Project Management*—This skill involves defining the project, determining how to solve the problem, allocating and ordering tasks, estimating time requirements, maintaining communication, and resolving conflicts.
- *Systems Perspective Taking*—This requires going beyond problem solving to understand why a problem arises and how it is connected to other problems.

I argue that team projects such as the one described in this chapter are extremely valuable for developing these kinds of competencies. I have found that it is helpful to make this case explicitly to students as well.

THE TEAM PROJECT

I have used a variety of semester-long team programming projects in the course CIS 403, Systems Programming and Operating Systems, at SUNY Potsdam. Each project is a complex, multistage assignment, chosen specifically to go beyond the ability of a single student, no matter how talented, to accomplish successfully. Teams, made up of three to five students, each work on the same project (a sample summary project description is given in Appendix I). Typically, the project involves designing and implementing a simulated multiprogramming operating system. The project extends for the duration of a fifteen-week semester, typically with six to eight subprojects due during the semester and the final program due at the end.

Almost all of the work of the teams takes place outside of formal class time, except on rare occasions. The class meetings themselves are run in a more traditional (lecture and discussion) manner.

Forming Groups

Students are permitted to form their own groups. Partially formed groups, in addition to students who are not able to find a group to join on their own, are assembled into complete groups by the course instructor. Permitting students to form their own groups has some disadvantages—for instance, stronger students tend to group together with other strong students and similarly for weaker students. Some groups, because of their composition, are almost doomed to failure without significant intervention from the instructor. Each group is responsible for selecting its own team leader to serve as a liaison with the course instructor, organize group activities, and act as spokesperson. Other defined positions that groups must fill are a backup leader and a documentation person who coordinates the project documentation and also ensures that everyone in the group is working with the most current versions of files.

In general, instructors should pay attention to how groups are formed and whatever procedures are used should be aligned with the goals of the course. Care should be taken to ensure that the group work will truly be a cooperative effort. David Johnson (1992) has pointed out:

> Many educators who believe that they are using cooperative learning are, in fact, missing its essence. A crucial difference exists between simply putting students in groups to learn and in structuring cooperation among students.... To be cooperative, a group must have clear positive interdependence, members must promote each other's learning and success face to face, hold each other personally and individually accountable to do his or her fair share of the work, use appropriately the interpersonal and small-group skills needed for cooperative efforts to be successful, and process as a group how effectively members are working together. These five essential components must be present for small-group learning to be truly cooperative.

One way the instructor can monitor group activity and stay on top of potential problems is to hold a weekly team leaders' meeting. These meetings tend to take place at the end of class or at a pre-arranged time (if possible). This technique has proven very successful in catching emerging problems at a stage at which intervention can make a difference. For instance, if the team leader reports that a particular team member is not participating in early team activities, the instructor can meet with this student and clarify his or her participation in the course.

Peer Evaluation

One of the most valuable exercises in the course is to have students evaluate the contributions of each member of their team to the overall team effort. A sample peer evaluation form is shown in Appendix II. Students are also given the option of rating themselves. The composite picture from these evaluations provides an instructor with rich feedback about each student's performance within the group context. It is interesting to see how consistent these evaluations tend to be within the group, as if there is a "group mind" that develops over the course of the semester. There are occasionally exceptions to this consistency when a student will have a completely different picture of the group members' contributions, usually with an inflated sense of his or her own efforts. However, I have found that most evaluations are pretty honest and accurate.

Project Evaluation

Each member of a given group receives the same group project grade, which typically contributes about 40 percent of each student's final course grade. Projects are graded on the following components: correctness (65 percent), documentation (15 percent), efficiency (10 percent), and maintainability (10 percent). An individual student's project grade is sometimes modified depending on the outcome of the peer evaluations. For instance, a team member whom everyone in the group rated an exceptional performer, but was part of a group that was not successful, would have his or her grade revised upward. Conversely, a team member whom everyone agreed was a weak contributor would have his or her grade revised downward, regardless of the overall team project grade.

Outcomes

The students describe this course and the associated team project as grueling, but also as a valuable and rewarding learning experience. Typically, a little more than half of the groups in any given semester are able to complete a fully operational project. All are able to demonstrate success on at least some of the subprojects. Students work hard on their projects and put in a tremendous amount of time, sometimes to the detriment of other courses that they may be taking. Students often plan their schedules so that they have a lighter load the semester they take "Systems." It is an interesting question to consider why students seem to be willing to devote so much more time and effort to a project like this than to their more typical class assignments.

Student project grades tend to align fairly closely with other class evaluations (e.g., in-class examinations), with some exceptions. Sometimes I have students who do exceptionally well on the project, but struggle with the more traditional class evaluations. Others are excellent students in the traditional sense (e.g., book learning and test taking), but have difficulty putting that knowledge into practice in the team context.

CONCLUSION

The intensive team project experience seems to be a transformative one for many students. Alumni of the CIS program at SUNY Potsdam often cite this course as the undergraduate experience they had that best prepared them for the world of work. It does seem that cooperative learning, structured as a team project, can be successful in preparing students with valuable competencies that will serve them well as college graduates.

REFERENCES

Brouwer, Peter. *An Analysis of Student Debugging Strategies.* Unpublished Ph. D. dissertation, SUNY Buffalo, 1993.
Johnson, David. *Cooperative Learning: Increasing College Faculty Instructional Productivity.* ERIC Digest ED347871, 1992.
Oblinger, Diana. "Hype, Hyperarchy, and Higher Education." *Business Officer*, October, 1999. Available at: http://www.nacubo.org/website/members/bomag/99/10/oblinger.html.

APPENDIX I

Sample CIS 403 Team Programming Project Description

MPX-PC (MULTIPROGRAMMING EXECUTIVE FOR PC)

Note: The CIS 403 programming project is a team project written in C. Teams will be made up of three to five persons. Students should attempt to form their own teams. If you cannot find or form your own team, you will be assigned to one.

A detailed description of the team programming project is given in the *Project Manual to Accompany A Practical Approach to Operating Systems,* by Malcolm Lane and James Mooney (PWS-Kent). What follows is a summary description.

There have been many attempts to provide a good project environment for studying operating systems. The project environment of *A*

Practical Approach to Operating Systems is straightforward and simple. The philosophy of the approach is that you will learn best if you are challenged to implement your own multiprogramming executive operating system project rather than simply studying or enhancing existing (real or instructional) operating systems.

To complete the MPX-PC project, student teams must complete a series of seven smaller programming projects. Once complete, teams will have a working multiprogramming executive (MPX) that runs on top of the PC operating system software. It is based on a model MPX operating system that has been developed by Malcolm Lane over many years at West Virginia University. Previous implementations have used several different computer systems. It uses a building block approach. Although each project appears to be a stand-alone project, most are in fact part of the larger MPX-PC project. Each stand-alone project can be independently tested because test programs that simulate the necessary MPX-PC environments (object modules) are provided to allow each component to be tested even though other related ones are not yet implemented. The final step in the approach is the integration of the modules into an operating multiprogramming executive.

The seven incremental projects are:

1. COMHAN—Command Handler
2. COMHAN Part 2—Process Management
3. Round Robin Dispatcher
4. COMHAN Process Management Commands
5. PC Interrupts/Clock Driver
6. Device Drivers
7. MPX-PC

A group approach has always been used to implement the MPX projects. This provides students with the experience of working in a group, but it also allows more "design and programming" power to work on projects. Over the years, we have found that a group of students has been able to produce the complete working MPX project (with documentation) far more easily than an individual student is able to.

APPENDIX II

Teammate Evaluation (Confidential)

The purpose of this exercise is to provide a peer evaluation of the contribution that each member of your team made toward the overall team effort. The rating you give should be based solely on the contribution each individual made to the success of the team.

Give each of the other members of your team an Overall Rating (Item Q) according to the following criteria:

Overall Rating	Description of Contribution
7	Contribution to the team was outstanding. Took initiative, did more than the average team member, and did work of superior quality.
6	Contribution to the team was above average. Did more than the average team member or did work of superior quality.
5	Always carried his or her fair share of the team's workload. Always produced work of good quality.
4	Usually contributed his or her fair share toward completing the assignment. Quality of work was mixed— some good and some average.
3	Made less than an average contribution to the project. Quality of work only average.
2	Contribution to the project was substandard. Depended on the rest of the team to do a large part of his or her work.
1	Made very little effort and produced poor work.

Name:

Team:

TEAMMATE EVALUATION

For A–M, indicate one of the following: E–excellent, AA–above average, S–satisfactory, BA–below average, P–poor
For Q, indicate (1–7) based on cover sheet Overall Rating

	Name #1:	Name #2:	Name #3:	Name #4:	Name #5:
KNOWLEDGE/ABILITY					
A. Knowledge of project					
B. Ability to analyze problems					
C. Ability to develop solutions					
D. Communcation ability					
ATTITUDE/MOTIVATION					
E. Desire to improve knowledge					
F. Willingness to accept responsibility					
G. Judgments and decision-making					
H. Effectiveness in working with others					
PERFORMANCE					
I. Completion of assignments					
J. Timely action					
K. Quality of work					
L. Quantity of work					
M. Participation in discussions					
Q. Overall Rating (1–7) (Scale from cover sheet)					

6

Combining Art Studio and Art History to Engage Today's Students

Caroline Downing
Art Department

Teachers of undergraduates often find themselves confronted with students who present two difficult problems: short attention spans and a profoundly visual orientation to learning. Most of today's students have, after all, spent many more hours watching television, playing video games, or surfing the net than they have reading books. They have developed as part of a visual culture unimagined when many of their professors went to school. That visual culture contributes to the formation of limited attention spans because its manifestations (think of MTV) feature fast-moving, brightly colored, and rapidly changing segments. The typical college lecture course, in comparison, cannot help but seem bland, colorless, and dull.

In my course called Landscape Art, I employ a method that enlists the visual to help students relate more closely to the subject matter. Landscape Art is one part of the interdisciplinary Adirondacks Coordinated Environmental Studies Program (hereafter referred to as Adirondacks) at SUNY Potsdam. Students in the Adirondacks program are first-year, first-semester students who take a group of courses that constitutes their entire course load. The number of students has varied from eighteen to fifty. Other courses in the Adirondacks program typically include environmental studies, Adirondack ecology, anthropology,

English composition, and environmental geology, all with an environmental focus. Often a physical education credit, such as an overnight backpacking trip, forms part of the schedule as well. All utilize the local Adirondack region of New York State, located just south of Potsdam's campus as their subject matter, laboratories, and outdoor studios. While our program is adapted to the Adirondack region, any region of the country could provide a focus for a combined art studio/art history course. I will elaborate on this later. In the Adirondacks program, Fridays are reserved for field trips, allowing enough time to travel and to study several subjects in the same day. For example, students may study the ecology of a stream in the morning and make a pencil sketch of it in the afternoon.

In Landscape Art, students study the history of landscape painting and create landscape art as well. All the students are first year, as mentioned, and few, if any, are prospective art majors. Many have no experience or background in art, and neither is required for them to enroll in the program. In the art history portion of the course we focus on nineteenth-century American artists, particularly those artists who worked in the Adirondacks. These include many well-known artists, such as Winslow Homer, Frederick Remington, Thomas Cole, and Rockwell Kent, as well as lesser known regional artists. The class meets twice a week for an hour and a half. Each class includes a short art history presentation, and then a studio art assignment. Students learn to draw and to paint in watercolor as a way of reinforcing what they learn in the art historical sections of the class. Early in the semester we study the visual elements and principles of design used to create works of art, looking at such topics as balance, color harmonies, and so on. After each of these early classes, we go outside and sketch trees, and students learn to put these ideas into practice. When you finally realize that the top of your tree is not going to fit onto the paper as you had planned, you have demonstrated in your own work the importance of balance and positive and negative space in a work of art.

By the time we begin to discuss landscape painting in depth in the art history presentations, students are beginning to create their own landscapes. They now have a much deeper understanding and appreciation of the task of painting as a result of active involvement in creation. For example, when we are learning about the influence of European landscapes on American artists, we look at the principles used by the eithteenth-century French painter Claude (Lorrain), such as framing the landscape with trees, asymmetrically arranged. Not only can students begin to see the use of these principles in American paintings, they can also employ them in their own landscape drawings and paintings. Moving from passive listening to active practice, too, helps alleviate the problem of the short attention span.

For their final watercolor painting, students are given a choice: to create a landscape in the Romantic tradition of Europe and the United States or one using the principles of Asian landscape painting. By this point, we will have looked at the Romantic tradition and the meanings of "sublime," "beautiful," and "picturesque" as they apply to landscape painting. It is their task then to bring one or more of these concepts to life in their own paintings. Study of Asian landscapes opens the students' eyes to new ways of looking at artistic interpretations of nature. Many are surprised to learn that perspective, for example, is not a universal scientific "given," but a cultural creation; students learn to recognize isometric perspective and multiple perspective in Asian landscapes, and to incorporate these into their own landscapes created in the Asian tradition. Having some choice helps students assume more control over the course assignments, and enables them to feel more committed to successful completion of their paintings. And since these are not art majors, having a choice allows them some feeling of control in an area over which most begin with little or no mastery.

For the last part of the semester, students work on other aspects of the art of the Adirondacks. Two studio assignments given late in the semester involve an Adirondack house design and an Adirondack garden plan, both following class presentations on architecture and the history of garden design in Europe and the United States. For the house design, we learn about architecture and its integration with the local environment, focusing on the principles of Asian domestic architecture and on Frank Lloyd Wright's house designs for different geographical areas of the United States. By this time, students have visited at least one Adirondack Great Camp, a rustic lodge designed for wealthy vacationers, and can incorporate rustic elements, such as rough-hewn logs and native-stone fireplaces, into their designs if they wish. When designing their Adirondack gardens, students must consider which plants can survive in the region, and decide whether to espouse the principles of the "natural garden" (only native species) or to use imported plants as well. As can be seen, both projects encourage students to use knowledge from their other courses, such as biology and geology, in an interdisciplinary way that helps them see connections between art, science, and culture.

A field trip to a museum with a large collection of landscape paintings is an important part of the class. Students in the Adirondacks Program travel to the Adirondack Museum in Blue Mountain Lake, New York, which has a permanent gallery of Adirondack art along with displays on mining, hunting, recreation, and the like. Students bring with them a short essay on one of the works on display in the museum that they have read about and seen in a reproduction before the trip. Each student prepares a written essay and then gives an oral presentation to the group. They are asked to describe their reactions to the differences they notice while viewing the actual work. Often, they are surprised by the differences in color, size, texture, and so forth between the reproduction and the actual work. This essay prepares students for a longer art historical paper at the end of the semester. Our location near Canada's capital city, Ottawa, allows us to visit a major city museum, the National Gallery of Canada, as well. At the National Gallery we hear a presentation from a gallery staff member on Canadian landscape painting using works of art from the Gallery's extensive collection of Canadian art. Students can then relate the subject and style of these paintings to those created by American artists.

Although today's students are visually oriented learners, this does not mean that they are discerning and sophisticated consumers of visual culture. They may have been bombarded with millions of visual images, but they have rarely been taught to examine them critically. On the contrary, most are more like passive receivers of an overwhelming overload of visual information. Being taught to draw and paint helps to refine their visual skills, and learning art history begins to help them to "read" cultural implications in the visual.

To take them still further on this path, we spend a class analyzing advertisements with environmental themes. Students begin to develop a healthy skepticism when they view, for example, an oil company's advertisement that features nothing but a wide-eyed little girl surrounded by adorable furry friends. It's a first step in helping to understand how the visual is used to sell ideas (and ultimately products) to consumers. The class also helps to prepare them for their final studio project, which is to create a poster on an environmental theme. Often this theme, which they are free to choose for themselves, will relate to some aspect of environmental protection. Tying this to the art historical background, students are quite surprised to learn that it was American artists who, as early as the mid-nineteenth-century, were trying to alert their fellow citizens to the threat of environmental destruction. Students learn that today artists are still in the vanguard, concerned with the effects of pollution, dumping, and other environmental problems, and depict these in their artworks. Other artists, instead of creating works only for museum and gallery settings, use nature itself as a medium. Goldsworthy of Britain specializes in ephemeral sculptures of stone, leaves, and ice; Smithson creates giant earthworks of dirt and stone; Christo and Jeanne-Claude erect large-scale temporary art projects that are part of the landscape or cityscape.

For a final product in the art historical section of the class, students choose an American landscape artist and conduct library research. The purpose of the paper is to have the student determine the artist's attitude toward nature, based on both library research and the student's own examination and interpretation of the artist's works. Students learn to research and write competently on an art historical topic after having first been given a way of viewing art history from the point of view of a practicing artist. While they may still struggle to create a written product, the topic is made more approachable, understandable, and perhaps somewhat less daunting because of their experience as creators of art.

While my course is designed to take advantage of the local Adirondack region, it could be adapted for any geographic area. In the Midwest, courses could focus on regional artists like Grant Wood or on Frank Lloyd Wright's prairie house architecture. In the Southwest, local Native American artists could be the focus, or artists like Georgia O'Keeffe, who created stark renditions of the New Mexico landscape. Photographers and painters have long been documenting the majestic scenery of the western landscape. Local museums and exhibits could be used as resources if a visit to a major art museum is not possible. Studio assignments could also be easily adapted: house and garden designs for the Southwest would obviously involve a number of different challenges than those for the northeast woodlands. Other projects could be designed for specific locations: for example, students could study how the giant dams of the West have altered the landscape, and how artists have documented these alterations and peoples' reactions to them.

Introducing students to the study of landscape art by utilizing principles and exercises of both art studio and art history helps to keep students alert and interested. Because most are not art majors, they are frequently concerned that they will not succeed because they are "bad at art." But in learning some simple drawing and painting skills, they become more confident, and are able to apply what they learn to the sometimes difficult concepts taught in the art historical section. Conversely, having practiced creating landscape art themselves, students feel more confident conducting research and writing about art from an art historical perspective. By involving students in active production of a visual product after being informed by art historical information, I am hoping to take advantage of their highly visual orientations, and at the same time to assuage the problem of their short attention span.

7

You *Can* Teach a Rock New Tricks

Robert L. Badger
Department of Geology

Dear Uncle Jed,

Hi, How is it going? I just wanted to thank you again for helping me pay for school. It was a great idea to take that geology class. We went on a field trip the other day to check out a big fault zone. This fault is like a big cut in the earth with each side moving in a different direction.

Dear Uncle Dave,

Boy have I got a place for you. There is this place in Colton that I know you would love. The area is marked by beautiful scenery as well as many geologic features that you would be interested in. The river is part of the Carthage-Colton Mylonite Zone. There was a unique folding of the rocks around the fault that is obvious in many locations.

Dear Uncle Emmett,

How are you and Aunt Agatha? I hope you enjoyed your kayaking adventure down the Nile. Since we share a common interest in rocks, I wanted to tell you about an area right here in the North Country that has some interesting features. I recently went on a field trip to Stone Valley, which is near Colton, and it has some interesting geologic features. You probably didn't realize that a fault zone extended from there to Carthage at one time. Stone Valley is one place where you can still see the fault. It's not known for sure if it is a strike-slip fault, but it appears to have shifted or sheared to the left. You can actually see folds in the rocks almost like an S-shape. The heat and pressure had to be really intense to fold them. There was ductility in the rocks. You are able to see veins or dikes of other types of rock layered between the main type of rock. In the veins you can see conglomerates, which have a much coarser grained texture to them. Closer to the fault the rocks are more fine grained.

So begin the opening paragraphs of student lab reports for one of my introductory geology courses. Writing letters home for credit? Well, yes. Why not? Whatever it takes to encourage students to write and to *describe what they see.*

LET'S FAIL BEFORE WE BEGIN

When I was a freshman, my introductory geology class went on many field trips to look at rock outcrops and construct maps. For each, we had to write a lab report recounting what we saw and did. My creations were abysmal. I had not picked up on half of what the teacher had explained, and his interpretation was what I thought he wanted spit back at him. How could I possibly write something that the teacher would want to read? So I wrote tired, uninspired drivel, merely recounting a vague version of what the professor or teaching assistant had recited, without trying to analyze for myself what it was that I had actually observed. At the time I promised myself that if the roles were ever reversed, and I was the teacher, I would never subject my students to such tedious and pointless exercises.

Twenty years later I found myself in that position, educated beyond my intelligence, and with a class full of eager young students intent on learning a little geology. Of *course* I led field trips—I was trained as a field geologist. That's what most geologists do—go out and look at rocks. But for my first couple of years teaching, unless the trip was tied into a larger project, I skipped the write-up. Just enjoy the trip and learn was my philosophy. But when I asked some very broad essay questions on an exam—basically asking the students to tell me what they had seen, thereby giving credit to those who were on the trip and penalizing those few who had skipped—I got some non-answers from many in the class who had been there. Their replies reflected limited comprehension and poor retention. I had to do something better.

I wanted observation on their part, then interpretation, based not so much on what I had told them but on what they had seen. I didn't care if the interpretations were wrong. I wanted critical thinking about their observations. Most of all, I wanted good observations. Reluctantly, since I did not have any better ideas, I started asking for the dreaded lab report, with predictably poor results. The students were trying to write for the professor, they did not *want* to write for the professor. The students knew full well that they did not understand what they had seen in the field nearly as well as the professor, so there was a defeatist attitude toward a chore that had to be done. There was also no leeway for creativity. This was science, damn it: facts, figures, and observations, cut and dried. And of course only one interpretation, the *correct* one, the one the professor had only mentioned as a possibility after considerable badgering. This was not much improvement over no lab report. I had to do something better.

LETTERS HOME

Then I remembered my undergraduate economics class, and the papers that I had to write:

> Dear Uncle K,
>
> In your last letter you asked about the World Bank. Let me try to explain...
>
> Dear Uncle K,
>
> Thank you for the beer money. I'll put it to good use after this letter is done. You asked about the difference between stocks and bonds...

Good old Professor Craven and Economics 101, a nonmajor course for the financially inept. Every assignment came in the form of a letter from a fictitious Uncle K, asking us about some financial institution or monetary policy. Our assignment was to write a letter back explaining whatever old Uncle K had inquired about. I knew little about finance, and had no particular interest in it either, but I sure had a good time writing those letters. I would talk about the weather, a party, a geology field trip (these really did interest me), and then would settle down and try to write about the World Bank, stocks versus bonds, or whatever the subject. This was not a report to

Professor Craven, it was to my dear old Uncle K, and he didn't know diddly about the subject. So I really tried to explain it to him. I tried to put it in my own words, so that I understood it, too. To my surprise, I earned an A- in the course—not bad for a financially inept scientist-to-be. And I really did learn something.

Educators call this learning method third-person writing—writing to someone other than the professor. If students describe something to someone who has not been there, they will usually do a much better job of describing, which leads to better interpretation, and hence better comprehension. They also put it in their own words, instead of reiterating mine.

So I tried this method in one of my introductory nonmajors geology courses, and have since repeated it several times. The assignment is as follows:

"Who's paying for your college education?" I ask pointedly, before we head out in the field. They look rather startled at the forward question. I repeat my question, addressing students individually. "Josh, who's paying for your education? Mary, how about yours?" I move rapidly among the students, so as to not really put any of them on the spot, until one by one a few start to respond, mumbling something about parents, their own funds, student loans, etc. I shake my head, "No, no, no. Your parents lost all their money gambling in Las Vegas last fall. Don't you remember?" A few of the students start to catch on, and nod their heads. "No, your parents aren't paying a dime for this education. They would rather you went out and worked, to support them in their old age." Usually, a student will unknowingly provide my cue line, "Then who is paying?" "Ahh," I reply, "Remember that eccentric uncle who used to come around when you were a kid? The one who always had rocks in his pocket? What was his name? Uncle Ralph?" A few more students are catching on, and offer their own eccentric uncles' names. "Yeah, remember him? Well, he's funding your college education. All four years, including books and that occasional check for beer money." Now they've all caught on, something about the word "beer." I continue, "He's a geologist, working for the U.S. Geologic Survey. He doesn't have any kids of his own to send to college, so he's paying your way. His only stipulation is that you take a geology course. That's this course. And he wants you write to him occasionally to tell him about the geology class, particularly the field trips. He hasn't been here. You have to be his eyes. You need to describe what you see and explain what it means. Tell him what you saw; tell him what you did."

This is the same information I would be seeking in a lab report, but in the context of a letter to a third party, it works. Most students start with small talk: "How's Aunt Mildred," and so on. One very quiet student rambled for a page and a half about how great dorm life was. Another put his letter in an envelope, addressed to me, with a return address of "XXXX Nudist Colony," and elsewhere written on the envelope, "Thank you for your last visit. Membership card enclosed." But most settle down and talk geology. In their own words, in their own style, they describe what they saw, what they did, and what they think it means (i.e., how were these rocks formed?). If there is an assignment besides the letter, such as a map to produce or data to collect, that is included and described. Their descriptions are fair to good. There are plenty of misconceptions, and those I address in the next class. But I believe the response, the enthusiasm, and the quality of their geological perceptions is far superior to what I would receive if I merely requested a routine lab report. Uncle Ralph had not been there, so the students consciously describe exactly what they had seen and done, and offer a plausible, cohesive explanation that fits the data.

I should note that I do not do this in my upper-level courses. For the advanced classes, students are gathering technical data and using it in scientific reports; they are beyond the stage of writing letters home and need to be learning to write in a specific technical style. But for introductory courses, I have been very pleased with the results. Not all students respond well to this method of teaching, but most do. I was somewhat surprised to find that nontraditional students, older students returning to school after a hiatus since high school or after a first failed attempt at college, have also responded quite well to this teaching method.

A DIFFERENT AUDIENCE

The success of the letters home in lieu of the lab report led me to try this method of third-party writing for a more complex project. For several years I have been part of Potsdam's Adirondack Studies Program (see also the previous chapter by Caroline Downing), an interdisciplinary coordinated studies program involving a group of first-year students enrolled in the same five courses, all of which have two central themes—the Adirondack region of New York and the environment. Each year we have a mix of five courses, lately consisting of English composition, environmental studies, landscape art, Adirondack ecology, and environmental geology (my course). Over the eleven years that this program has been in existence, the ecology professor and I have developed a wonderful two-week lab project on a nearby stream. During the first week's lab, students are given a scaled base map of the stream, and are asked to map the stream features in detail. These include oxbows, rapids, channel bars, point bars, fishing holes, undercut banks, beaver dams, former stream channels, and so on. The students are then put into groups and each group is assigned a different section of the stream where they measure the chemical properties of the water—pH, nitrates, chlorides, phosphates, and total dissolved oxygen; they measure velocity and volume of flow, and also identify the plants growing along the banks.

During the second week's lab, each group returns to their assigned section of stream and spends a couple of hours using nets to collect all the aquatic organisms (stone fly nymph, water strider, caddis fly nymph, black fly larvae, etc.) and, using this data, determine species diversity. All this data is presented in maps, tables, charts, and diagrams as group projects, along with a write-up on the general health of the stream. After two or three years of rather mediocre reports, we changed the written assignment. Instead of asking for a scientific report, written for the ecology professor and me, we asked the students to pretend they were professional river guides, and had been sent to scout the river for potential rafting trips. This made most of the collected data relevant—sand bars were needed to camp on, fishing holes to help supply food, water quality became important for drinking and swimming, rapids and undercut banks needed to be noted for safety. As potential guides, they had to be educators for the paying public and able to identify the flora and fauna along and within the stream. All this was to be in a report sent back to the rafting company.

The papers we received were an improvement. No longer writing for us, many of the students did a credible job of describing the features of the river and citing their data to support their conclusions on the overall health of the aquatic system. This method was successful in accomplishing our goal of teaching the students descriptive analysis and   properly using their data for interpretation. But then, consciously, we changed our goal and abandoned the third-person method in favor of focusing on improving their technical writing skills by requiring them to write a real scientific report. The scientific quality of the reports has improved, which was our revised goal, but unfortunately their descriptions of the river and discussion of their field methods have noticeably deteriorated.

A Sense of Home?

Another writing exercise I frequently use is one I may have subconsciously adapted from a high school history class in which we had to write about what it would be like to have been a soldier in the Revolutionary War. Students are asked to transpose themselves in time and place to when the rocks in their hometown were formed, and to describe what the area looked like, using the first-person, present tense. This exercise comes after they have learned about geologic time, geologic maps, depositional environments, and a minute amount concerning the evolution of plants and animals through geologic time, so they know something about the first appearance of multicelled organisms, shelled organisms, land plants, organisms with backbones, trees, reptiles, bees and flowering plants (how could bees evolve 80 million years before flowers?), mammals, and so on.

The students find their hometown on the geologic map of New York, use the map to determine age of the rocks and their lithology (sandstone, shale, limestone, etc.), and then, from what they have learned about depositional environments for this type of rock, and organisms that evolved during this time period, write a short story about what it would be like to be there at that time. Would they be on a beach? In a swamp? In a warm shallow ocean? In a deep marine environment? What organisms might be swimming around? Or crawling on land? What plants, if any, were growing on land? I urge creativity.

One male student pretended to be a trilobite, a small marine organism that dominated the seas 400 to 500 million years ago, and talked about his mating call that "really attracted the babes." A week before he was clueless as to what a trilobite was or anything about the geology in his hometown. Another student took herself back in time with a mountain bike, describing what she saw as she rode around, really emphasizing how the rock outcrops in her backyard and along the road leading to her house had once been molten lava.

A third student wrote from the viewpoint of a bug living on the edge of a body of water:

Things were pretty calm for quite a bit of time, until...the Paleozoic Era. We all knew change was comin', it was in the air. Actually, it really was kinda high up in the air; the plants were growing these big chunks of wood off their stalks and trunks. It started pretty slow, so for a while it didn't hit us that these could be a bug hazard. But then it did hit us, it hit us hard. Well, actually it hit my friend Cort really hard; one of those suckers fell and drove him a clear 3 inches into the mud. We were so broken up about it that we named this whole place after him: 'Cortland.' Two weeks later the thing sprouted up from the ground into a new tree. We called 'em 'seeds' on account of Cort hadn't 'seed' 'em coming.

REFLECTIONS ON LEARNING METHODS

It is hard to measure the success of these writing methods as teaching tools. I know I am more satisfied with the results than I was before I initiated them. In the letters home, the descriptions and observations were what I wanted to stress and these were vastly improved over the basic lab report. Some students have really enjoyed playing along, continuing the concept into the classroom: "Professor, I got a call from Uncle Ralph last night. He was wondering if you could explain..."

When the third-person target writing method was adapted for the larger project, it worked as long as our goal was to improve their observations and descriptions. But when we changed our focus and decided to emphasize technical writing, it no longer served our purpose, so we readily abandoned it.

The third case, when I ask the students to transport themselves back in time, is an assignment still evolving. My goal is their realization that the land is constantly changing. By recognizing that their hometown was once a swamp, shallow ocean, beach, or part of a long eroded mountain range, I hope to impress this concept of a changing landscape on them. Their creativity often emerges after they understand the concept, but sometimes it emerges before, and I get descriptions of events that just are not possible. Despite BC Comics and my son's eigth grade science teacher, at no time did human beings and dinosaurs share this planet, yet this has come through on a paper or two. Similarly, the Finger Lakes of New York, carved by glaciers during the past 2 million years, have also shown up in writing as witnessing the evolution of trees, some 350 million years ago. This assignment comes up in only the third week of class, so I am not overly concerned about the confusion of evolutionary events, but the juxtaposition of events that happened tens or sometimes hundreds of millions of years apart is something I need to eliminate from this assignment.

Why do such assignments seem to work, when the student knows full well that the teacher will be the one reading and grading the paper, not a fictitious uncle or a trip planner for a rafting company? In his book *Teaching with Writing*, Toby Fulwiler discusses the concept of an audience other than the teacher. He points out (49) that when a student is writing for the professor, "The teacher's superior knowledge precludes the student's writing out of any real concern for communicating or sharing knowledge with the teacher." Instead, Fulwiler suggests that in order for the student to want to communicate new information, in my case to describe and try to interpret observations, the student needs an audience "that wants to learn or needs to know something." And here is where dear old Uncle Ralph and Aunt Bertha enter the picture.

> Dear Uncle Ralph,
> Just writing my weekly update. How's Aunt Bertha's back? Has Grandpa come yet?
>
> Well, on with business. In Geology class last Thursday we went on a trip to South Colton to make a map of a rock formation. I have sent a copy of my map with this letter.
>
> When we arrived, our professor gave us some background of the area. He told us that the rock we were standing on was a gneiss that is over one billion years old!! Tell Grandma that; she will undoubtedly make a joke about Grandpa's age. He also told us that the rock was probably originally a sedimentary sequence that got buried and was heated at a temperature of approximately 650 degrees centigrade. The minerals quartz and feldspar would have melted first. As they melt, they migrate upwards forming veins and pockets known as pegmatites.... Overall, Uncle Ralph, this was a pretty interesting day. Seeing examples like this firsthand really gives me more of an understanding of how these things were formed.
>
> —Your favorite niece

REFERENCE

Fulwiler, Toby. *Teaching with Writing: An Interdisciplinary Workshop Approach*. Portsmouth, NH: Boynton/Cook Publishers, 1987.

8

Blinded by the Light: A Reflection on the Teaching of Introductory Courses in Philosophy

David Curry
Department of Philosophy

I must confess from the outset that I have nothing new to say here. What I do have to say has all been said before, and, no doubt, said better. The same can also be said of my undergraduate introductory philosophy courses, in which nothing new is ever really said. They consist of little more than a rehash of oft-repeated conversations from classrooms, salons, and marketplaces throughout the ages. Nonetheless, I do not apologize for saying these things yet again. Though I am humbled by the recognition that I have nothing to add, I still remain sufficiently unlearned to hold back from repetition.[1]

The justification for such repetition arises from the continued frustration professors often express concerning what they take to be the limited success of their introductory classes. Why aren't our classes opportunities to present the latest philosophical theories, to present our own new and bold theses, to dispute the big questions of existence, the real stuff of philosophy? That they are not such opportunities needs, I take it, no argument. Though somewhat depressing, reality demands that we acknowledge that to expect them to be would be (at least at a small sort-of-state-supported public liberal arts institution like

Potsdam) to set unreasonable goals and expectations for an introductory course in philosophy.

Consider our students: They are, in short, a mass of latent contradiction and tension: a fertile field of potential confusion ready for the harvest. They have absorbed the ubiquitous moral puritanism of our society along with the equally ubiquitous commercialization of sex and violence. They live in the most widely touted democracy in the world, in which oligarchs and corporations compete for leadership and set the social and political agenda. They live in the largest secular and multicultural society in the world, yet retain a puritanical provincialism and a naive spiritualism. They are raised in a world made by science, yet place their hope in psychic hotlines and the power of crystals to heal. They are individualists who just happen to all wear the same brand of jeans. They are moral relativists who are proud to proclaim their allegiance to the universal moral truth du jour. They are already a bundle of confusions and contradictions, though they are also, amazingly, completely unaware of the fact. They take it for granted that they are savvy, skeptical, clever, and informed when their entire educational history up to the day they enter our classrooms has almost certainly been little more than teaching facts to the tests, and has certainly not required subtlety of thought, has discouraged any sort of mitigated skepticism, has impeded cleverness, and has, at best, kept them minimally informed by convincing them to take mainstream commercial media as their sole source of information. Equally amazing is the fact that some of them have actually survived this process, or at least are salvageable.

Our students are also, notoriously, 'unprepared' to engage in college-level work, which is a nice way of saying that they are strikingly uneducated, on the whole. This sad fact alone, combined with the intimate relation that philosophy has to its own history, makes it clear why it would be unreasonable to have particularly high aspirations. One cannot understand the latest philosophical theories without being able to set them in the context of the history of philosophy, something few introductory students are equipped to do. So, too, to properly argue for and defend any of one's own philosophical beliefs ethically entails that one argue them out against competing hypotheses and theories, something that our students are even less prepared to do. Philosophy is a dialectical process, an ongoing conversation, and like other conversations it is tough to pick up the thread when suddenly dropped in the middle of it all. Not that there is any alternative. Still, although like Hegel's non-swimmer on his first attempt, there is no other way to learn to swim than to plunge on in; nonetheless, one should not expect much in the first few dips—a dog paddle in this context can be pretty impressive. Finally, to properly dispute the big questions of existence, my students would need to have some basic grasp of the process and rules of argumentation, and, alas, I cannot even count on this. So given the latent confusion of my students and their general state of intellectual unpreparedness, aiming to present new and bold theses or opening serious disputations concerning the big questions of existence would be to aim unreasonably high. Does recognizing this condemn the introductory philosophy class to merely rehashing well-worn material along well-trod paths? What might be justification enough to walk yet again over these roads? Does this undermine the whole enterprise? What should we, or can we, reasonably strive to achieve?

Retreating from the clearly unreasonable, one might try to take up a kind of middle ground. Certainly, we might say, students should come away from an introductory course with an understanding of why and how philosophy has been done, an appreciation of the methods and conclusions of three or four diverse thinkers, and improved critical thinking skills. What are the chances of achieving even these modest goals with a significant portion of introductory students? While trying desperately to remain realistic and not give in to the temptations of free-wheeling cynicism, I must still reply that the chances of achieving such goals are slim indeed.

Withdrawing a bit further, perhaps I might hope that in five or ten years my students will look back on their foray into philosophy with a solid understanding of at least a handful of issues of central philosophical concern, the intellectual desire to pursue others, and the kind of critical engagement required by an active citizen. But this is still wildly optimistic. Perhaps these latter goals might be reasonable for those who pursue extended study or a major in philosophy, but, even then, it is only the best and the brightest who will come anywhere near achieving them.

So what can one reasonably hope to impart in an introductory philosophy class? Having held the dragons of fantasy at bay and, I hope, equally avoided the pits of cynicism, I have come to believe that the best method of introducing students to philosophy is to promulgate confusion. That is, I set out to make difficult and confusing what was before deemed untroublesome. My goal is to create, disseminate, share, and foment confusion. We might call this a process of active unlearning.

Preposterous, one might say. What kind of a discipline, particularly when introducing itself, would pursue such seemingly irrational ends? What kind of a professor professes confusion? Isn't our purpose, as teachers, to shed light on the obscure and misunderstood: to make clear and help to order the chaos of our experience? I do not deny that these are noble and admirable goals. We should enlighten where we can, but to teach we must understand. If you are like me in this respect, there is much that we do not understand. Across our various disciplines and areas of expertise we all have much light to shed, yet we also all find ourselves on occasion, at least, blinded by that very light. We spend much of our time dazed and confused (and if we didn't, many of us would seek other means of employment!). The life of the mind is not placid and clear, it is a "buzzin' bloomin' confusion." Introducing students to that confusion and modeling for them the ways of negotiating that confusion, I am arguing, is a responsible and reasonable goal. Perhaps even noble as well.

The idea is a very old one, however, and again I must confess that I have little or nothing new to add to it. But ideas do not have a shelf life, and even if pushed to the back and ignored, forgotten, or eclipsed by some new and improved reworking of the old product, they are as good as they ever were, and cannot reasonably be dismissed merely on the basis of their age. Thus, predictably, unimaginatively, unoriginally, but I hope not unhelpfully, I suggest we take a look at Socrates.

Plato's Socrates famously asserted, "wondering: this is where philosophy begins and nowhere else." (*Theaetetus*, 155d). The context of the passage suggests wonder, not, for example, over the mysteries and beauty of the natural world, or even of the moral world, but rather wondering of a purely intellectual variety over some rather obscure 'logical' (strictly, I suppose, epistemological) puzzles. Theaetetus expresses his 'wonder' (*thaumas*) over how it can be that three seemingly self-evident principles can conflict when applied to certain common cases in experience.[2] And the terms of his expression are equally revealing, for he says, "I often wonder like mad what these things can mean; sometimes when I'm looking at them I begin to feel quite giddy" (*skotodineo*: to feel dizzy or vertigo) (155c7–8). Now giddiness is not a state normally associated with the experience of the wonders of nature and art. It is much more naturally associated with another psychic state also commonly associated with the name of Socrates—namely, *aporia*, the state of being at a loss, confused, or perplexed. Plato portrays the historical Socrates as engaged in conversations about moral issues that always, without exception, end in *aporia*; that is, without having answered the fundamental question that the inquiry set out to answer. This is certainly explicable by reference to Socrates' profession of ignorance, but this still leaves room for us to see in it a clear pedagogical end as well.

Socrates' all-too-evident failure to get answers to the questions he pursues, to educate himself, is itself ironically transformed into an opportunity for his interlocutors to educate themselves: to come to see puzzles and difficulties where before there were none. Socrates is, as Meno suggests, constantly in danger of being "driven away for practicing sorcery" (*Meno*, 80b8) for carrying on in this way. Socrates' goal is moral improvement, both his own and others. But he first has to get them to see that there are moral difficulties at all, get them to appreciate that, echoing Nietzsche, thinking about morality might be difficult and dangerous. And to this end he sows confusion, *aporia*. For millennia, for the receptive reader, at least, he has provoked wonder in the form of confusion and perplexity.

Socrates always began his examinations by asking a question about something he had reason to believe the person with whom he was speaking might know about. Inevitably, they would reveal in their answers that they knew less than they let on. Of course Socrates' standards may have been set unreasonably high, but they are conducive to sowing confusion, and thus serve a distinct pedagogical end. The other Socratic gem, from the *Apology*, is the claim that "the unexamined life is not worth living." Taken literally (as it must be, though rarely is), this is a rather harsh claim. For when we unpack what Socrates means by examining one's life, it will appear that most of my students' lives are not worth living, and some of the rest of us might bear it heavily in mind as well. For it precisely means that a worthwhile life requires that one be constantly checking up on one's beliefs, particularly one's moral beliefs, subjecting them to a kind of eternal recurrence of cross-examination. This few manage to achieve (arguably, Socrates himself may well have failed), but for the majority of undergraduate students the question is not one of the constancy of their examination, but of its ever having begun at all. All I can hope to accomplish in one short semester is to get them to see that there is a way of living that involves dedication to such questioning.

To achieve this end, I become a Proteus, now defending the plausibility of Descartes' arguments, then that of his critics, weaving a maze for those interested enough to puzzle their way through. They don't follow, of course, and I don't really mean for them to. Simply opening the door and letting them look into the labyrinthian passages is shock enough, like that suffered by the prisoners in the cave who first turn to face the wall on which images of the real are paraded. The more engaged among them ask questions, pursue ideas, and I support those ideas, help them think through them, or show that they are insupportable. Whether we are discussing Cartesian dualism, Sartre's conception

of freedom, the morality of abortion, or the limits of our First
Amendment freedoms, this is critical thinking in action, the give-and-
take of reason and argument. They are having it modeled for them and
a few actively take part. But this is more active unlearning than active
learning. Their conceptions of things are more often undermined than
they are supported. In a straightforward way, they leave the classroom
knowing less than when they entered.

Lest I be misunderstood, it is important to point out here that confusing is not simply 'problematizing' in the postmodern sense, since it
must clearly imply that there is truth to be found. It is true, as so often
put forward by the postmodernists, that things are much more complex
and ambiguous than they may seem. And certainly it does our students
good to come to appreciate this. But to conclude from this that truth is
relative would be a classic non sequitur. Nonetheless, many students
will interpret the give-and-take of arguments, the demand for vigilant
skepticism and for open-mindedness to be evidence for their crude rela-
tivistic views. Part of the task, then, is to get them to see that this
doesn't follow. To put them on the road, at least, to coming to see for
themselves that this is precisely the sort of inference about which they
should be skeptical and which requires reexamination.

To return, predictably, to Socrates, it would be wrongheaded to
conclude from the fact that his conversations (charitably so-called)
always end in *aporia* and therefore the real lesson we are meant to
draw from them is that there is no truth about the matter being discussed. Indeed, Socrates himself spends time addressing this wrongheaded conclusion in the *Phaedo* and warning his listeners about the
dangers of what he calls "misology" or hatred of argument.

> "You know," he says, "how those in particular who spend
> their time studying contradiction in the end believe themselves
> to have become very wise and that they alone have under-
> stood that there is no soundness or reliability in any object or
> in any argument, but that all that exists simply fluctuates up
> and down as if it were in the Euripus [a violent and variable
> current] and does not remain in the same place for any time at
> all" (90b9).

Yet it would be pitiable, he goes on to say, for such people to place
the blame on the arguments or on reason itself, rather than on themselves or their own lack of skill. Pitiable, because they would thereby
deprive themselves "of truth and knowledge of reality." Thus, "we
should not allow into our minds the conviction that argumentation has
nothing sound about it; much rather we should believe that it is we

who are not yet sound, and that we must take courage and be eager to attain soundness" (90e1).

In short, nobody said discovering the truth would be easy. Indeed, it requires hard work, perhaps the work of many lifetimes. Nor can it simply be handed from one individual to another. They must come to make it their own, and thus they, too, must work themselves to it (not surprisingly, one theme in operation in Plato's *Meno*). These points, although they are old hat, are received like foreign delicacies by our students. They live in a quick fix, value meal, Cliff-noted, and Internet-referenced age. They expect truths to be delivered to them, preferably via multimedia. What, after all, are they paying their tuition dollars for? This is an attitude that has been reinforced, in almost all cases, by twelve years of public schooling, and which will continue to be reinforced by many of their undergraduate classes.

Confusion as the end or goal they find to be, well, confusing. It is not facility of mind they have been encouraged to develop. Thus, active unlearning should for some of us be a goal, if only because it is so rare and yet so necessary. It takes on more importance in the teaching of some disciplines precisely because it is so rare in others; because it challenges the educational norms students have been raised within, and, perhaps most important, because it is so alien to the corporate mentality, and hence to the dominant ethos of our age. Only from the point of view of an authoritarian, political/corporate culture can questioning the status quo, sowing confusion, be seen as harmful. But so it is seen today, as it was in Socrates' day. We have no less, and perhaps much greater, need of a gadfly today than Athens did 2,500 years ago. And the place for such gadflies in the diffuse and massive society that is contemporary America is not in the marketplace, but in the university.

In Socrates' day the market was a place where people could mingle and explore ideas together. Today the market actively seeks to thwart the exchange of ideas and to discourage the sowing of confusion. The market, as has often been noted, does not merely seek to supply our wants, desires, and needs; more than ever it creates those wants, desires, and needs, and seeks to homogenize them at the same time. The market is perhaps inescapable; we are all consumers. But as consumers we require the tools supplied by active unlearning to keep from being manipulated by the market. And the area of our lives as consumers in which we now are in need of the most active, critical thinking and skepticism is in our role as citizens. As the political process becomes more and more a matter of marketing a product, democracy itself becomes endangered by the dearth of critical thinkers, of gadflies, and by the legions of those who have only learned and never unlearned.

And though many, myself included, are heard to bemoan the quality of the students who now enter our classrooms, this decline of quality is directly correlated with a larger percentage of the general population who now go on to pursue an undergraduate degree. Jackson Lears has noted that "professors are constantly berating themselves and being berated for withdrawing into the insular world of scholarship, for not connecting with the real world. The real world is right in front of us, in the classroom; it is composed of students, 99 percent of whom have no intention of entering the academy themselves. They are a non-academic audience; they require us, however implicitly or imperfectly, to become public intellectuals." (2000, 22). As teachers working in a small state university, we know all too well that the real world is right in front of us. We are all public intellectuals, whether we like it or not. Certainly, directing the light where we can is required of us, but so is making certain that our students, our audience, are blinded by the light as well, introducing them to the kind of *aporia* Socrates radiated. The opportunity being presented to some of us is to spread confusion far and wide, to get our students, a sizeable portion of the adult population, thinking about issues they had never even imagined could be troublesome or difficult. It is, admittedly, arguable whether even this can be achieved in a few short weeks, but it is our obligation, as public intellectuals as well as active citizens, to at least try. And when my students come to me at the end of the semester and tell me that they are now more confused than ever about what they do and should value, I can take comfort in knowing that I have attained some small measure of success.

Notes

1. In part this is because I maintain that some things are worth repeating, even if only in a rather shoddy way. Socrates suggests in the Phaedo that there are some beliefs of such importance that they should be reinforced by repetitively working through them "as if it were an incantation" (114d5). As I understand this claim, Socrates is comparing the belief to the product of the incantation, and the incantation itself represents the giving of reasons, the premises of the argument. Hence reinforcement, in this case, is equivalent to reexamination. The belief he is reexamining there, of course, is the belief in the immortality of the soul.

2. The principles are:
    1. that nothing can become greater or less, in bulk or in number, while remaining equal to itself.

2. that if nothing is added or taken away from a thing, it can neither increase nor decrease but can only remain equal.
3. that it is impossible for a thing to ever be what it was not
   before except through a process of becoming what it was not
   before.

These principles cause problems when applied to common cases. So I, who haven't grown or shrunk an inch (i.e., have neither increased nor decreased) will soon be shorter than my eldest son; as the fifty cents in my pocket is larger than the twenty-five cents in my daughter's pocket and also, without having changed at all (while remaining equal to itself) is smaller than the ten dollars in my middle son's billfold. That is, these seemingly self-evident principles run into difficulty when applied to what we might now call "relational" properties. This is, of course, the kind of problem only a philosopher might wonder about, because only a philosopher might try to find a problem where others see only self-evident principles.

References

Cooper, John, Ed. *Plato: Complete Works*. Indianapolis: Hackett, 1997.

Lears, Jackson, "The Radicalism of Tradition: Teaching the Liberal Arts in a Managerial Age." *The Hedgehog Review* 2 no. 3 (2000).

9

Through the Comfort Zone or Just One More Go at College Teaching

Oscar Sarmiento
Modern Languages

> I suspect we teachers sometimes use our students' supposed unpreparedness for controversy as an excuse to avoid it ourselves.
>
> —Gerald Graft

Of political leaders, as we know, people expect courage to lead. It is a given that political representatives must excel at the difficult craft of political negotiation. They are to take into account all the players' interests and be inventive enough to arrive at negotiated resolutions for the good of the people. For this very reason, to catch political leaders holding their ground and taking a stance that may affect their popularity ratings is inspiring and healthy. Granted, this move does not have to be a turning point in their political careers; a worthwhile statement that speaks truth to power in an everyday situation is all that counts.

In what follows I would like to argue that, not unlike political representatives, concerned college professors actually endeavor to shape and bring in a splendid democratic, inclusive approach to bear on complex, difficult issues. More important, perhaps, we struggle to find ways to break free from that pleasing and teasing comfort zone we find ourselves easily encapsulated in because we want to take on healthy risks while at the same time secure productive learning environments. Perhaps these days our teaching practice in the classroom has become particularly challenging because, if we are to trust in Gerald Graff's words in *Beyond the Culture Wars. How Teaching the Conflicts Can Revitalize American Education,* "The expansion of the student body to include large numbers of students from non-traditional backgrounds (a process still far from completion) has been taking place at the very moment when the academic disciplines have become more wide-ranging and less restricted by their traditional definitions" (91).

But no matter what, we know that by taking risks and challenging students to unravel what at first may seem obscure and absurd, we help them navigate that experimental and experiential terrain where cultural boundaries are felt to clash and shed light on each other. People certainly expect college professors to be in command of their own disciplines and to have the courage to teach and "make it new" (poet Ezra Pound's dictum) by displaying new means to safely push open the limits. According to Gerald Graff, "Good teachers, after all, want their students to talk back. They know that student docility is a far more pervasive problem than student intransigence. Good students for their part appreciate teachers who take strong positions on controversial questions — though they do not appreciate brainwashing" (9).

By unlearning well-trodden teaching routines and thriving in learning from stepping into messy newness, I would argue, our teaching becomes the most exhilarating experience at hand. After all, even if we would like to do away with controversy so as to play it safe and avoid the embarrassment of uncertainty, differences do play a key role in a democratic learning process. Graff, again: "It is time to recognize that arriving at consensus is not the only way to pull a curriculum together, that difference can be a basis for coherence if it is openly engaged rather than kept out of sight" (58). Paradoxically, we do not enjoy the excitement of this ambivalent terrain unless we carefully prepare the classroom to take a turn that may seem uncertain at first, but proves to be a truly productive one after a while.

Sheila Tobias argues that "one of the reasons we did not ask enough questions when we were younger is that many of us were caught in a double bind between a fear of appearing too dumb in class and a fear of being too smart" (62). How much of this fear transfers into the college classroom at our institution we keep assessing, I am positive, in each of our teaching sessions. And time and again, to our good fortune, the spark of an unusual perspective, the challenge of a non-anticipated student question that seemed to be perhaps the least likely kind of question he or she could formulate, turns out to be a key that unlocks a constellation of responses and formulations the whole class could not quite anticipate coming down their way. What seemed unnecessary, idle, and perhaps fruitless, achieves articulation and significance in the act of producing together a response that not only and simply "makes sense" but adds another, unique dimension to our collection of inquiries. And this is made possible by a respectful intellectual learning environment that serves as a springboard for unsuspected explorations. As Robert Leamnson stresses: "If they are to be 'led out,' (e ducere) students need a clear picture of where they are, and where they ought to be" (54).

This is even truer of SUNY Potsdam students because we still find that a significant number of them need steady encouragement to trust that their own experiences and reflections matter, have an impact, and thus accept the fact that they can also be openly and surreptitiously challenged in the classroom. As Henry Louis Gates, Jr. puts it, "College isn't kindergarten, and our job isn't to present a seemly, dignified, unified front to the students. College students are too old to form—we shouldn't delude ourselves—but they're not too old to challenge" (118).

On the other hand, I surely wish we could find a magical formula to keep a class session from losing its precious intensity and edge. The fact of the matter is, however, that there is no ultimate trick, no simple teaching redemption for a dedicated college teacher. Time and again, day after day, we walk the walk through the halls of the college (we surely would like to spray with at least some flashy, Grateful Dead colors), quickly saying "Hi" to colleagues and students; we keep walking the walk toward the classroom to catch at least some glimpse of that sweet teaching interaction that thrives in producing positive knowledge exchange. If we only could less temporarily convey the intellectual excitement we once felt upon uncovering some paradoxical formulation that in our disciplines made us thirsty for further explorations of the same kind. This excitement parallels to me that moment in which, as Walter Benjamin has it, one seizes "hold of a memory as it flashes up at a moment of danger" (255). Benjamin's highly condensed sentence articulates with precision the fleeting nature of that precious creative dimension we seek to unfold, display, and share in the classroom — that dimension that will get lost if we, as an active community of learners, do not make our move fast enough to capture it and learn from it.

For instance, the delicate task of making a creative connection between language signs, processing information in unexpected ways, altering one's way of thinking and speaking by learning, for example, the vast, unknown territory of a second language, requires the unlearning of a number of routines that secure us against the ground of "normalcy." And when the ground begins to shift under our own very feet, we come to the realization that our perceptions need revision and more sophistication. As Jacqueline Jones Royster points out, "We need to get people out of central territory so that they can see what's really there and not there, so that they can see that even people who take tremendous comfort in occupying central territory show evidence themselves of distinctions that are worth noting—if we are ever going to recognize that there is no such thing as a generic human being, a generic American, or a generic student. Even when we look pretty much the same, we're not" (147).

In *A World of Difference* Barbara Johnson writes about the need to activate our own ignorance so that it becomes a tool for learning and, I would add, teaching something that matters: "If I perceive my ignorance as a gap in knowledge instead of as an imperative that changes the very nature of what I think I know, then I do not truly experience my ignorance" (16). When students are most in need of unpacking their minds of the contradictions and struggles that energize contemporary culture, when they feel the urgency to question what has become monotonous and simply repetitive, the traditional understanding of ignorance as a gap in knowledge plays it safe for them. This blindness toward the critical potentiality of our ignorance formulates questions and delivers answers without attempting to cross the many thresholds that in today's global society a college level class is most in need to endlessly navigate. As we know, when students learn something valuable, something that is truly relevant, it radically affects their perceptions and values. (Un)learning, therefore, has to include this core radical component, this alteration of perceptions to make of the students' college experience something worthwhile and endearing.

While teaching that discomfort matters, then, students and faculty need to keep alert so as to infuse our classrooms with enough room to make a moment of awkwardness into a turning point for a teaching "revelation." Obviously, this possibility gets most easily dismissed when a cunning authoritarian practice of teaching prevails inside the classroom. In his satiric book *La oveja negra y otras fábulas* (The Black Sheep and Other Fables), noteworthy Central American writer Augusto Monterroso has depicted a telling class situation that, I believe, summarizes the bleakest possible educational scenery both institutions and teachers dread and strive to avoid at all costs.[1] In his fable "El Grillo maestro" ("Mr. Cricket, the Teacher"), the principal of a local school enters a classroom while Mr. Cricket, who was teaching the art of singing, tells his students that

> the Cricket's voice was the best and the most beautiful among all voices because it came about after rubbing one's wings against one's sides, whereas the Birds were singing so poorly because they kept trying to sing through their throat, obviously the least indicated organ in the human body to produce sweet and harmonious sounds. (my translation, 201)

As in many of Monterroso's fables, humor here issues from the plain absurdity of the character's statement. Monterroso highlights the contradiction between the analytical language the teacher displays and the absurd foundation of his reasoning. In this class situation, Mr. Cricket's language is validated by his status as a teacher (and at least his gender and age) and by the school administration that has placed him in the position to instruct the younger crickets. The pomposity and complacency of Mr. Cricket's approach to teaching reveals itself in full when at the end of the story the reader finds out that, "upon hearing that, the Principal, who was a very old and wise Cricket, assented several times with his head and left the room, satisfied that in his School things were still running as smoothly as in old times" (my translation, 201). This kind of indoctrination that pretends to pass by teaching would be too apparent were it not for the proper command of the official "educational" language Mr. Cricket exerts to lecture the little crickets. His sharp explanation by contrast and comparison attests to the fraudulent but fairly savvy strategy the teacher utilizes to carry on the school's message.

The tragic moral of Monterroso's fable is, in the end, that Mr. Cricket will keep repeating the same "truth" with the same assertive voice inflection, convinced that there is no more logical or more profound explanation someone could produce in class to his students. Thus, his absurd statement on singing will continue dazzling the audience so that neither Mr. Cricket nor his students will ever get to question such comforting ground of trite ideas. His performance as a teacher will thus keep winning over more partisans for a "noble" cause.

Fortunately for us, Monterroso knows best, and through his relentless satire tells the same story anew, deconstructing the very mechanisms that enforce blindness and strive to dilute actual insight. As Barbara Johnson would most probably argue, ignorance as a gap places us back in that comfort zone where a critical attitude toward knowledge vanishes and a prescriptive attitude substitutes for an alert pedagogy that allows students to think critically through fruitful disagreement. And as Gerald Graff argues in "Organizing the Conflicts in the Curriculum," "When truth is contested, it is by entering into debate that we search for it" (138).

To do away with moments of friction, discomfort, and awkwardness would be deadly for the learning process that needs to take place inside our classroom. Securing enough room to preserve these moments as instances of new revelations based on mutual trust, encouragement, and civility is the least we can do at the college classroom level. New beginnings start at the rough core of our courage to teach, our courage to learn and unlearn.

NOTE

1. I will be quoting from Monterroso's *Cuentos, fábulas y lo demás es silencio*. This collection includes, among other books, *La oveja negra y otras fábulas*.

REFERENCES

Benjamin, Walter. *Illuminations*, Hannah Arendt, ed. New York: Schocken, 1968.

Gates, Henry Louis. *Loose Canons. Notes on the Culture Wars*. New York: Oxford University Press, 1992.

Graff, Gerald. *Beyond the Culture Wars. How Teaching the Conflicts Can Revitalize American Education*. New York: Norton, 1992.

Graff, Gerald. "Organizing the Conflicts in the Curriculum." In *Slevin's Critical Theory*: 125–139.

Johnson, Barbara. *A World of Difference*. Baltimore: Johns Hopkins University Press, 1987.

Leamnson, Robert. *Thinking about Teaching and Learning*. Sterling, VA: Stylus, 1999.

Monterroso, Augusto. *Cuentos, fábulas y los demás es silencio*. Mexico DF: Alfaguara, 1996.

Monterroso, Augusto. *The Black Sheep and Other Fables. Tales Wry, Sly, and Truly Fabulous*, trans. Walter I. Bradbury. New York: Doubleday, 1971.

Royster, Jacqueline Jones. "Literature, Literacy, and Language." In *Slevin's Critical Theory*: 140–152.

Slevin, James F., and Art Young, Eds. *Critical Theory and the Teaching of Literature. Politics, Curriculum, Pedagogy.* Urbana: National Council of Teachers of English, 1996.

Tobias, Sheila. *Overcoming Math Anxiety.* New York: Norton, 1993.

10

From the Traditional Lecture Toward Dialogical Learning: Changing Patterns in the Teaching of History

Ronald Woodbury
Department of History

History is the forty-nine-and-a-half minute lecture. The natural sciences have their laboratories. The arts have their studios. Philosophy and literature are text-centered. Political science and sociology are in the same lecturing tradition, but the parent of both is history. In no other discipline is the tradition of faculty standing before students to tell them information so deeply rooted.

The problem is that lecturing is poorly attuned to learning. The very word "lecture" comes from the Latin, *lectio* or *lector* for "reading" or "reader" and suggests its medieval origins in a pre-Guttenberg time when teachers read to their students because the students could not buy the hand-scripted texts of the day. But even if you could get any two historians to agree on the same story for a given subject, history is not a story, a mere narrative of names, dates, and places, to be transferred from faculty brain to student brain. History is interpretation of the meaning and significance of the past, not the past itself. It is inevitably about alternative interpretations and for that, fundamentally dialogical, best understood through an interactive process of testing and refining ideas. To teach history as a one-way process from professor/scholar/authority to ignorant student is to obfuscate, to pretend away, how historians actually work.

I say forty-nine-and-a-half minutes because the classic lecture in history, as still delivered by most history faculty, ends with the clock edging to the end of the period and students edging out of their seats. Teachers no more seriously expect a student to ask a real question (as opposed to "Is this going to be on the exam?") than a student (other than that one brilliant one who doesn't care what other students think) would risk the wrath of his or her compatriots by actually asking a serious question and thereby delaying the end of class.

Faculty know all this; they really do. Each of the students in my U.S. history survey courses has to read and report on an article by an historian writing professionally to other historians about a controversial topic in American history. They find the assignment very difficult and dislike most of all the way the historian will start out by going on and on about what all these *other* historians have said about the subject. The students sometimes have trouble even figuring out where the other historians leave off and the one they are supposed to be reporting on actually says what she or he thinks. But perhaps for this they get the point that real history, the history that is interpretation of the past as opposed to the recitation of names, dates, and places, is always interactive and dialogical—and often controversial.

This is the point at which most of the new faculty being hired in our department begin. From there, rethinking teaching and learning is not about pedagogy, although it probably does derive from some increased emphasis in graduate schools on the idea that teachers should think about how students learn instead of just how faculty might tell students what they should know. Heaven forbid to most arts and sciences faculty, it is not about "methodology" as they assume (incorrectly on the whole) the dreaded Education faculty think about learning divorced from content. Rethinking teaching and learning is about recognizing history as essential to the liberal arts because history, by focusing on differing but legitimate interpretations, liberates students from ignorance, narrow-mindedness, and prejudice.

RETHINKING THE LECTURE

Recognizing that the standard lecture often fails to engage the minds of even good students busily copying down everything the teacher says, is not to claim that the solution is to abandon it completely. I spend one-quarter to one-third of my class time highlighting key events and ideas. Even a class that is primarily lecture, moreover, can benefit from devices that break it up and engage students:

1. Halfway through your class, stop and ask students to write down one substantive question—they will learn over time the kind of question you mean—responding to the material you have presented. Yes, that would mean limiting or truncating your grand ideas that *require* forty-nine-and-one-half minutes to explain, but you have to ask yourself whether it is better to have fewer points that students have some grasp of or all the points you want to make but that mostly go over their heads.
2. Even better, have each student discuss his or her question with another student nearby.
3. Have groups of students agree on one "good" question and get one or two groups to ask theirs' out loud. One reason students do not ask questions individually when asked to is that they are understandably afraid of asking a "dumb" question. At least if it is "our" dumb question, they do not feel so at risk.
4. Collect the questions, without names on them, to get a better sense of how you are actually communicating your ideas.
5. An alternative to questions is one-sentence statements of what the students think your main point is. (Talk about revealing!)
6. Finish the lecture, taking what the students have said into consideration.

This can be scary. One reason teachers lecture is that it is ground that they totally control. It may be why the practice has held on for so long in the face of overwhelming evidence from Alexander Astin and others that it does not work very well to promote student learning of either the subject matter or larger general education goals like understanding others or participating in community activities.

As soon as you open your classroom to serious dialogue that recognizes the legitimacy of ideas worked up by students, there is no putting the genie back in the bottle. Students may raise questions you never thought of. They may disagree with you, causing you to defend your point of view and, heaven forbid, even revise future lectures. Especially if your course is part of a learning community, they may bring with them the legitimization that comes, as two students of mine recently did, from opening their statement with, "Dr. _____ in my Politics class said.... " (In fact, I had *never* thought or heard of the idea presented— and said so. It was also a very interesting point.)

ALTERNATIVES TO THE TRADITIONAL LECTURE

At the center of the transformation of teaching among new faculty in our department is the primary document. Use of primary documents is by no means new, but allocation of significant periods of introductory course class time to student discussion and reporting on primary documents is. Teachers assign students to read primary documents outside of class in order to discuss and report on them in class. Students use them for in-class debates and systematic analysis through a series of questions about a document.

It is essential for effective student discussion of, and reporting on, any kind of historical material that, at least initially, students have a well-defined task to accomplish, most typically a series of questions to which to respond.

My classes, like many of my colleagues', include simulations, debates, films, oral presentations, and especially small-group discussions and reports on issues discussed in class and based on homework already done. In-class small-group discussions allow students who would not participate as individuals in a teacher–student dialogue to feel free to speak in the small group. Psychologically, just as it is too risky to ask questions in lecture, it is just too risky for most students to offer their opinions in open class based on their own knowledge alone. Once part of a group, their opinions are subsumed in the group and, however erroneous they may be, are at least the group's opinion, not just one individual student's.

Students who would never talk in class talk in small groups. Sometimes these students are strong ones who regularly do their home-work. But others who would not otherwise complete their homework are at least more likely to do so when they are expected to work with other students in class. I try not to embarrass students in front of their peers, but peer embarrassment is not without value.

WRITING AND CRITICAL THINKING

All my U.S. history survey classes are also first-year writing and critical thinking courses. That is, they meet the general education requirements for writing and critical thinking just as do composition courses in the English department. This dual objective of teaching history and critical thinking fits well with the notion of history as primarily about interpretation of the past and enables me not only to focus students on historical interpretation and argument but also to involve them as groups in active consideration of historical issues. Thus, partway through the semester, they are working on a five-paragraph persuasive essay about whether the Constitution of 1787 made the country more or less democratic. Each must do a draft essay with peer assessment of the papers according to the following criteria, adapted, with some additions, from Sheridan Baker's book on persuasive essay writing, *The Practical Stylist*:

1. At the top of the first page, is there a clear statement in your own words of the question to be answered?
2. Is there a *strong title* conveying the subject matter and, ideally, the direction of the argument?

In the first paragraph:

3. Is there an *"invitation"* and *"funneling down"* to the thesis statement, ideally at the end of the paragraph?
4. Is there an *assertion*, stating the basic argument, opinion, point of view?
5. Does it *acknowledge the opposition*, suggesting at least some *evidence* for an argument "con"-trary to the writer's argument? [called the "con" argument.]
6. Does it give *reasons*, suggesting, by topic, idea, or fact, the *evidence* that the writer is going to present to support his or her argument?

The second paragraph:

7. Does it, with a *topic sentence* and *transition*, develop the evidence of the argument *contrary* to the author's, which is the argument to be rebutted?

The third and fourth paragraphs:

8. Do they, again with a *topic sentence* and *transition*, rebut the opposition "con" argument, and develop and support the main argument, covering at least the main points suggested in the thesis?

The fifth paragraph:

9. Does it restate the main argument/thesis/assertion/conclusion and funnel out to the implications of the argument?

Overall

10. Is the argument logically developed with supporting evidence from the text or other sources?
11. Does the paper evidence good sentence structure, word choice, grammar, and spelling?

Each student reads at least one other student's paper, critiquing it according to these criteria and discussing it with the writer. Collectively, the group to which they belong chooses a paper on which to report. Clearly, the level of student critique varies but, through writing and discussion, the process does result in students participating in analysis of the ideas of the course.

USING PRIMARY DOCUMENTS

As an example of what my new colleagues are doing, one has an in-class exercise called "Reconstructing Reconstruction." Dividing his class into five groups, he gives each group a couple of contemporary Thomas Nast cartoons to examine. The students are to explain the issues raised and figure out what Nast was trying to say. Each group has different cartoons. Each has a spokesperson chosen to report to the class as a whole. As the students report, my colleague scribbles their ideas on the board in "brainstorm fashion."

One group has cartoons illustrating the need to punish the South and ensure the rights of freedmen; a second group's cartoons decry the Democratic Party's resistance to black rights, depicting a coalition of northern capital, the Irish, and unreconstructed southerners; a third group's cartoons focus on the corruption of Horace Greeley; a fourth's Nast's dim view of black voters; and a fifth's Nast's disillusionment with the Grant administration and what he saw as the ultimate failure of Reconstruction. As each group reports and my colleague outlines their conclusions on the board, he notes that "a history of Americans' perceptions of Reconstruction is created as that history unfolded."

Another new colleague uses short homework assignments to address such questions as "Consumerism and American Values," "American Imperialism," and "Affirmative Action and the Culture Wars." As an example, for the consumerism discussion, she asks students to "write five sentences explaining five values you see expressed in the sources... then write five sentences explaining the most important means presented by the advertisements to reach each of the five values... [and finally] group every source that you think illustrates those means under each sentence." For class discussion, students explain what the products and advertisements tell about the historical era and compare those of the turn of the century to "our own era." This process she sees as telling about the "values—hopes and fears—of the people buying the products or, at least, the hopes and fears the advertisers thought the buyers would have." "An advertisement of today," my colleague says in her assignment, "might suggest freedom as a value and travel as a means to express that freedom."

In the end, there is no right way to involve students in historical interpretation and analysis, but cumulatively the many ways faculty in our department are choosing to involve students is a challenge to the traditional lecture as the only means of teaching and learning in history. In the end, the multivariate approach even impacts the fifty-minute lecture format as more and more teachers request more flexible seventy-five-minutes classes. The forty-nine-and-one-half minute lecture is no longer the given it once was.

REFERENCE

Baker, Sheridan. *The Practical Stylist*, 8th edition. Boston: Addison-Wesley, 1998.

11

Preparing Teachers to Use Technology in the Elementary Mathematics Classroom

Sergei Abramovich
Teacher Education

Computer as Alternative Teaching and Learning Tool

One of the central tenets of the current reform movement in mathematics education holds that appropriate use of tools of technology is integral to the teaching and learning of mathematics at all grade levels. A major force in this reform, the National Council of Teachers of Mathematics (NCTM), strongly believes that placing a high priority on the development and implementation of instructional materials that capitalize on the unique power of these tools can advance the excellence of the curriculum and improve the quality of students' learning (NCTM, 1989, 1991, 2000). The introduction of computers into schools was followed by a trend toward seeing technology as a crucial factor in restructuring schools (Johnson, 1997). This put mathematics content and pedagogy for pre-service and in-service elementary teachers (hereafter referenced as teachers) in a unique position because technology-driven changes must be feasible from the very outset in the chain of children's educational experiences. The challenge for mathematics teacher educators is to make a computer a useful learning tool, a powerful mediator of meaning-making processes in the elementary mathematics classroom.

Another noteworthy focus of reform is the continuous growth of teachers as technologically informed professionals. Such growth implies that teachers are given an opportunity to gain awareness of using computers to pursue mathematical explorations and investigations. Current thinking in this area is that the integration of computers into teacher education programs should emphasize learning with technology versus learning about technology (Garafalo, Drier, Harper, Timmerman, and Shockey, 2000; Shaw, 1997; Willis, 2001). This implies that the focus of the integration of computing technology into mathematics education courses for teachers should be the use of a computer as a cognitive tool rather than as a delivery system. The proficiency of teachers in using of a computer as a tool for their own conceptual development and educative growth becomes an important factor in advancing such use with younger children. Furthermore, coursework for teachers should include true experiences in designing technology-integrated lessons that focus on the exploration of a mathematical content, search and interpretation of patterns, and computational problem solving.

There is a sense of agreement among mathematics educators that computing technology is a remarkable agent of reform. Technology fosters learning environments in which a student's growing curiosity can lead to the discovery of significant mathematical ideas. Technology enhances mathematics learning, supports effective mathematics teaching, and influences what mathematics is taught (NCTM, 2000). Technology brings about the dynamic perspective on mathematics through reformed teaching. To make technology integration into a quality teacher education program a success, the choice of software for mathematics education courses becomes a crucial issue.

Frequently, when one talks about software as a mathematical/pedagogical tool, one means a program designed for a particular educational purpose. Yet economic constraints often stand in the way of incorporating special purpose software into an instructional setting and thus challenge computer-mediated mathematics pedagogy and ongoing in-service and pre-service programs. A possible way of addressing the financial challenge is to shift emphasis from specific computer applications as teaching and learning tools to a broader and more sophisticated use of general-purpose software. For example, a spreadsheet is a highly popular tool for computations outside the domain of its original design and it is commonly available in schools, colleges, and universities.

That spreadsheet software was singled out as an appropriate tool for *doing* mathematics as early as in grades 3–5 (NCTM, 2000) is most likely due to the remarkable applicability of spreadsheets to the teaching of a broad range of topics in mathematics, including those appropriate for younger children (Abramovich, 2000, 2003; Abramovich, Stanton, and Baer, 2002; Ainley, 1995; Ainley, Nardi, and Pratt, 2000; Drier, 2001; Dugdale, 1994; Fuglestad, 1997). Students at the 3–5 grade level are expected to acquire ability to set up a simple exploratory spreadsheet in their mathematical pursuits and to "use it to pose and solve problems, examine data, and investigate patterns" (NCTM, 2000, 207). In this recommendation, one can recognize the above-mentioned shift toward the use of generic software tools in mathematics education. Furthermore, one can appreciate such a shift as a timely contribution to the important objective of egalitarian education—universal access to technology regardless of socioeconomic status of students and schools (Shaw, 1997).

The content of this chapter reflects on my work with teachers enrolled in several computer-enhanced mathematics education courses (including one entitled *Using Spreadsheets in Teaching School Mathematics* and *Creative Problem Solving*) at SUNY Potsdam over the last several years. It argues for the integration of spreadsheet-enabled and open-ended pedagogies as a strategy to enhance the learning of mathematics by teachers at different levels of sophistication. Through mathematically and pedagogically appropriate use of the software, teachers develop as technologically minded reflective agents (Cooney, 1994), capable of appreciating technology-enabled mathematics pedagogy as a field of disciplined inquiry. Most important, teachers become skillful in incorporating spreadsheets into the practice of mathematics teaching. My experience indicates that, in many instances, the technological amplification of an open-ended pedagogy is conducive to presenting mathematics to teachers as meaningful and motivating subject matter, something one would ultimately enjoy teaching to younger children.

SPREADSHEET-ENABLED PEDAGOGY AS A SOCIOCULTURAL PHENOMENON

The appearance of computers as alternative instructional tools has not only opened up significant educational opportunities, but also has created new didactical problems. Due to its name, a computer is often construed as an innovation that brings a change to the subject matter from a computational perspective alone. While computers do aid in computation in many powerful ways, such utilization of technology in a mathematics classroom can further perpetuate authoritative discourse (Bakhtin, 1981). Such a discourse is grounded into an unconditional acceptance of one's word (whether the word of a teacher or a verdict of a computer) without any attempt to reflect on its meaning or to modify its semantic context. In the elementary mathematics classroom, authoritative discourse focuses on the mastery of small isolated computational steps aimed at only 'one correct answer.' A static meaning structure of 'right or wrong' evaluations generated by a computer is unlikely to be taken as a thinking device by a student. Yet, an egalitarian, student-centered, and meaning-making pedagogy is the focus of the current mathematics education reform. The principal assumption of such an alternative pedagogy dwells on the notions of reflective inquiry, dialogic discourse, and conceptual development. In this tradition, the quality of the educative growth of a student is measured in terms of the quality and diversity of thinking rather than in terms of the production of correct answers (Dewey, 1926).

As far as a spreadsheet as a learning environment is concerned, it is not immediately apparent how it could be put to use so as to challenge the conventional belief that there is only one way or the best way of acting and representing in the context of the structurally robust body of mathematics. Indeed, in a seemingly contradictory computer-entrusted situation, teachers are encouraged to manifest open-ended pedagogy and promote internally persuasive discourse. The lack of instructional materials and paucity of pedagogical precepts concerning the alternative use of computers make the incorporation of technology into mathematics teacher education courses an important issue.

Nevertheless, the appropriate use of spreadsheets in such courses enables an alternative pedagogy that can be conceptualized along the lines of what Wertsch (1991) termed a sociocultural approach to mind. This approach assumes that individual mental functioning is inherently situated in a social context within which learning occurs through action mediated by cultural tools. Such an action can generate signs that, in turn, can be used to create new tools. Thus, it is useful to single out a semiotic mediation as being relevant to school mathematics discourse with its emphasis on concrete materials, pictures, diagrams, tables, and graphs (NCTM, 1991).

The major claim of socio-cultural approach to mind is that the semiotic as well as other forms of mediation shape human action in many important ways. For instance, pictures, cartoons, and diagrams have a potential for creating a context for the transition from concrete to abstract reasoning; mnemonic strategies and questioning techniques can mediate the recall of information. Thus, the term "mediated action" reflects the fundamental relationship between the action and mediational means it employs. Any mental action directed toward solving a mathematical problem and mediated by appropriate tools and signs may be termed a mediated mathematical action. An illustration in the next section shows how spreadsheets can mediate mathematical action by providing a tool kit of diverse semiotic devices.

Another basic principle associated with the sociocultural approach to mind is that human mental functioning originates in the course of communication and thus is inherently social. In a particular sociocultural setting, a contemporary elementary mathematics classroom, a mediated mathematical action can be grounded in the appropriation of the tools of technology such as computers and semiotic devices such as mathematical symbols and notation systems of the software used. The goal of an instructional discourse in such a setting is to use the mediational means as generators of meaning that, in turn, shape mathematical action.

From the sociocultural perspective "any true understanding is dialogic in nature" (Voloshinov, 1973, 102), and this claim ties meaning closely to the dialogic orientation of the discourse. As far as an introduction of a computer into the discourse is concerned, it is of paramount importance to provide an environment capable of engaging the student into a purposeful dialogic encounter with the computer. This kind of an encounter encourages the student to reflect the computer's response to his or her mathematical action. Here, a classroom pedagogy is focused on the reduction of an authoritative discourse in favor of a dialogic discourse, which, according to the sociocultural conceptualization of learning, awakens new meaning for a student.

AN ILLUSTRATION: AN INCORRECT ANSWER AS A THINKING DEVICE

As an illustration of a spreadsheet-enabled nonauthoritarian discourse, consider the following scenario grounded in a long-established tradition of using grids for the study of the concept of percent by shading parts of a grid in a given percentage. In particular, such grid-based percentage tasks are recommended by the New York State Education Department (1998) as appropriate paper-and-pencil activities for the elementary level. The capability of spreadsheets to serve as a manipulative-computational environment enables these tasks to be interactive. That is, any iconic structure created by a student on a spreadsheet can be connected computationally to the numeric domain. It is this interactivity of spreadsheets that makes it possible to move beyond the authoritarian pedagogy of 'right or wrong' evaluations and in doing so to use an incorrect answer as a thinking device.

More specifically, consider a spreadsheet-based 100-cell grid pictured on the left-hand side of Fig. 11.1. A teacher initiates an activity by shading a certain number of cells on this grid. The student's task is to decide what percent of the grid is shaded and reply by entering his or her percentage number into an answer box (a cell of the spreadsheet). The hot link established between iconic and numeric notations of the environment enables a computer to display a message evaluating the content of the answer box. If the student's answer is incorrect, a computer-generated message suggests continuing the task on an otherwise hidden identical adjacent nonshaded grid. The objective of this new task is to give a student an opportunity to use an incorrect answer as a thinking device and, in so doing, to shade a region on the adjacent grid that does correspond to the incorrect answer. In other words, the didactic emphasis of the task is to prevent undesirable consequences of a negative evaluation and to allow for the latter to awaken new meaning for a student.

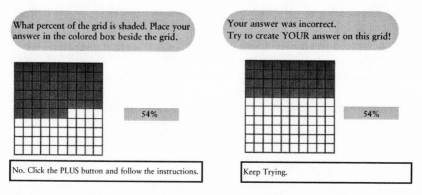

Figure 11.1. Incorrect answer as a thinking device.

This pedagogy is aimed at establishing symmetry between the last two phases of the Initiation-Reply-Evaluation didactical triad (Mehan, 1979). Traditionally, a negative evaluation of a student's response to a teacher's question contributes to the stretching of asymmetric relationship between the two parties. The importance of evaluation, however, as a fundamental component of teacher–student interaction suggests extending its notion to accommodate classroom pedagogy shaped by an internally persuasive discourse. Whereas a positive evaluation is likely to be considered as a terminator of a learning activity in an assertive sense, a negative evaluation can be introduced into an internally persuasive discourse as a mediator of a student's reflection on the activity.

By turning an incorrect answer into a self-generated task, this use of a computer spreadsheet encourages a student to reflect on an earlier answer through the active construction of his or her original guess within a computer-mediated environment. As Figure 11.1 shows, mathematical action on the right-hand grid is mediated by interactive messages like "Keep Trying." In such a way, negative evaluation can be considered a kind of a positive intent since it has a potential to function as a thinking device and generator of new meaning. This illustration is just one example of using a spreadsheet in a dialogically oriented classroom. Other examples may include the use of interactive spreadsheets in the study of the four arithmetic operations (addition, subtraction, multiplication, division), geometry (symmetry, area, and Pythagorean triangles), combinatorics (permutations and combinations), and fundamentals of number theory (divisibility, factoring, primes, and polygonal numbers).

TEACHERS' VOICES FROM A COMPUTERIZED CLASSROOM

One of the factors supporting current mathematics education reform is the recognition of teacher education as a field of disciplined inquiry. Mathematics education research suggests that the way teachers learn mathematics affects the way they will teach it, something that, as Cooney (1994) observed, was ingeniously missing in the reform movement of the recent past. Nowadays it has become generally accepted that researchers in the field "appreciate the blurring of content and pedagogy...because...what we learn is encased in how we learned it...[and] think of the teacher as an inquiring mind rather than as the object of an inquiring mind" (627). With respect to the technological component of mathematics teacher education research and development, such shift in the emphasis of the reform efforts highlights the importance of analysis of how teachers' views of mathematics and its pedagogy change, evolve, and mature throughout their pre-service and in-service professional development. Another important question that arises here is how the use of technology affects teachers' belief systems regarding the relationship between mathematics and its pedagogy.

My experience indicates that learning to retrofit spreadsheets into an elementary mathematics classroom can be backed up mostly by the teacher's excitement about its great potential as a mathematical/pedagogical tool. An in-service teacher who had begun one of the technology-

enhanced mathematics education courses with only basic word-process-
ing skills affirmed that a limited computer background "has not dimin-
ished my excitement and enthusiasm of the potential use of technology
in my classroom." In her opinion, using technology in teaching mathematics to children "parallels the development of mathematics itself over
the centuries. From manipulative, to pencil and paper abstract notations, to using these notations (formulas) to generate information on
the computer, I believe the children need multiple experiences to understand these complex relationships." In particular, looking forward to
teaching mathematics with spreadsheets, the teacher acknowledged, "I
am especially excited that my school is purchasing a portable large
screen which I can use in the classroom for demonstration purposes.
Even though the students will not be at computers themselves they can
come up and shade in the grids to answer the questions. My kids really
like this! "

It should be noted that all information regarding syntactic versatil-
ity of a spreadsheet as well as mathematical/pedagogical demonstrations can be introduced to teachers not as a final product but in real
time, allowing their active involvement in a discourse on syntax, content, and pedagogy of a particular environment. That is, teachers can
experience teaching with technology not through authoritative discourse but instead through multivocal egalitarian conversation about
the birth, development, and implementation of the ideas. It is this intellectual milieu that allowed one teacher to remark, "I enjoyed our class
discussions on [spreadsheet] formulas as we were able to try out and
see the results immediately." Indeed, the classroom where the course
was conducted had a computer for demonstration purposes that was
available for anyone who wanted to try his or her own ideas in front of
the class.

It appears that the level of mathematics preparation of elementary
teachers has a direct dependence on the increasing use of technology in
schools. Frolic effects of interactive computing, multicolored icons, and
the ease of using sliders by younger children do not diminish the importance of the teacher's knowledge of the subject matter as some chal-
lengers of technology-based instruction might allude. Quite the
contrary, as my experience indicates, the use of spreadsheets by teachers is likely to positively affect their general perspective on the study of
mathematics. According to one teacher, "The use of a spreadsheet further broadened my understanding of alternative modes of teaching
rather than just lecture and hands-on busy work. It also gave me a
better understanding of some interesting concepts discovered many
years ago." The teacher goes on to assess the relationship between con-

tent knowledge and technology-enhanced pedagogy: "I feel teachers must have more knowledge of the subject matter so that they can keep the child focused and challenged at all levels. I see the computer in the classroom as a friendly tool for the students, not just a time filler."

This point was further advanced by another preservice teacher: "Briefly working in the spreadsheet environment it becomes obvious that it is more important today that universities provide our upcoming teachers with a strong background in mathematics so they would feel comfortable to sort through the open-ended character of the computer environment." In her opinion, "the limited comfort level with mathematics of many elementary school teachers has limited our American children's achievement in this area." This teacher believes that the advent of spreadsheet-based environments into schools calls for a better conceptual understanding of mathematics on the part of teachers: "What was a deep concern in the past really becomes a critical issue with using a spreadsheet as mathematical/pedagogical tool."

One of the major advantages technology brings to the elementary classroom is the emergence of an open-ended intellectual milieu that allows for a variety of ideas to be explored. In such a setting, a teacher's role becomes one of extreme complexity, for she or he is simultaneously substituted by a computer as an external authority for validation of truth and required to be an adaptive and reflective partner in advancement, capable of surviving ambiguity in a meaning-generative dynamic environment. Thus, teachers' attitude toward the so-structured didactical setting may provide an additional insight into one's conceptualization of new patterns of interaction between content and pedagogy.

For example, one in-service teacher believes that "open ended pedagogy is an essential component in a mathematics classroom. Many times a child will pick up on things no one has ever noticed because they are not as tied to viewing the world through the constraints which sometimes limits the views of a more educated person. It is always a joy to view the world through the eyes of a child! Our educational system often is a study of what mankind has learned in the past, and we, teachers following the tradition, try our best to organize and present this body of knowledge to the next generation. Mathematics, however, is a dynamic discipline and must be presented to students as such. We must not restrict their young minds." This is in agreement with another in-service teacher opinion about patterns of interaction shaped by an egalitarian classroom discourse: "Students can become interested and want to explore an avenue or branch of the assignment that the teacher may not have thought of before. Students may inherit enthusiasm not only from the teacher but other students. This [open ended] environment definitely allows for creativity."

The voices of teachers from a computerized classroom indicate their potential to move the field of mathematics education toward realizing the high visibility of the NCTM Principles and Standards for mathematics taught in schools. Many comments made by teachers manifest their potential to be reflective and adaptive, capable of understanding how younger children "come to know and believe what they do" (Cooney, 1994, 628). Developing such ability in teachers is one of the fundamental goals of contemporary mathematics teacher education.

REFERENCES

Abramovich, S. "Mathematical Concepts as Emerging Tools in Computing Applications." *Journal of Computers in Mathematics and Science Teaching* 19 no. 1 (2000): 21–46.

Abramovich, S. "Cognitive Heterogeneity in Computer-Mediated Mathematical Action as a Vehicle for Concept Development." *Journal of Computers in Mathematics and Science Teaching* 22 no.1 (2003): 29–51.

Abramovich, S., M. Stanton, and E. Baer. "What Are Billy's Chances? Computer Spreadsheet as a Learning Tool for Younger Children and Their Teachers Alike." *Journal of Computers in Mathematics and Science Teaching* 21 no. 2 (2002): 127–145.

Ainley, J. "Re-viewing Graphing: Traditional and Intuitive Approaches." *For the Learning of Mathematics* 15 no. 2 (1995): 10–16.

Ainley, J., E. Nardi, and D. Pratt. "The Construction of Meanings for Trend in Active Graphing." *International Journal of Computers for Mathematical Learning* 5 (2000): 85–114.

Bakhtin, M. M. *The Dialogic Imagination: Four Essays by M. M. Bakhtin*, ed. M. Holquist, trans. C. Emerson and M. Holquist. Austin: University of Texas Press, 1981.

Cooney, T. J. "Research and Teacher Education: In Search of Common Ground." *Journal for Research in Mathematics Education* 25 no. 6 (1994): 608–636.

Dewey, J. *Democracy and Education*. New York: Macmillan, 1926.

Drier, H. S. "Teaching and Learning Mathematics with Interactive Spreadsheets." *School Science and Mathematics* 101 no. 4 (2001): 170–179.

Dugdale, S. "K–12 Teacher's Use of a Spreadsheet for Mathematical Modeling and Problem Solving." *Journal of Computers in Mathematics and Science Teaching* 13 no. 1 (1994): 43–68.

Fuglestad, A. B. "Teaching Decimal Numbers with Spreadsheets as Support for Diagnostic Teaching." In M. C. Borba, T. A.Souza, B. Hudson, and J. Fey, Eds, *The Role of Technology in the Mathematics Classroom* (pp. 79–89). Proceedings of Working Group 16 at the 8th International Congress on Mathematics Education, Rio Claro, Brazil, State University of São Paulo, 1997.

Garofalo, J., H. Drier, S. Harper, M. A. Timmerman, and T. Shockey. "Promoting Appropriate Uses of Technology in Mathematics Teaching." *Contemporary Issues in Technology and Teacher Education* 1 no. 1 (2000). Online serial: http://www.citejournal. org/.

Johnson, D. L. "Integrating Technology in the Classroom: The Time Has Come." In D. L. Johnson, C. D.Maddux, and L. Liu, Eds, *Using Technology in the Classroom* pp. 1–5. New York: Haworth Press, 1997.

Mehan, H. *Learning Lessons.* Cambridge: Harvard University Press, 1979.

National Council of Teachers of Mathematics. *Curriculum and Evaluation Standards for School Mathematics.* Reston, VA: NCTM, 1989.

National Council of Teachers of Mathematics. *Professional Standards for Teaching Mathematics.* Reston, VA: NCTM, 1991.

National Council of Teachers of Mathematics. *Principles and Standards for School Mathematics.* Reston, VA: NCTM, 2000.

New York State Education Department. *Mathematics Resource Guide with Core Curriculum.* Albany, NY: NYSED, 1998.

Shaw, D. E. *Report to the President on the Use of Technology to Strengthen K–12 Education in the United States.* Washington, DC: President's Committee of Advisors on Science and Technology, Panel on Educational Technology, 1997.

Voloshinov, V. N. *Marxism and the Philosophy of Language,* trans. L. Matejka and I. R. Titunik. New York: Seminar Press, 1973.

Wertsch, J. V. *Voices of the Mind: a Sociocultural Approach to Mediated Action.* Cambridge: Harvard University Press, 1991.

Willis, J. "Foundational Assumptions for Information Technology and Teacher Education." *Contemporary Issues in Technology and Teacher Education* 1 no. 3 (2001). Online serial: http://www.cite-journal.org/.

12

At Home in the Universe

Lawrence P. Brehm
Physics

There are several important aspects to learning physics, as well as teaching it, that pertain mostly to those who will eventually put it to professional use, to those seeking to become physicists or to use physics in engineering or other work. Among those aspects is the experimental part in which learning how to use a lathe, solder a wire connection, or mix a solution may be all-important. There is also the learning of particular methods of analysis, which could include anything from mastering a computer language to solving a particular type of mathematical equation to operating an elaborate laboratory instrument.

My interest and purpose here are more general. What follows are some thoughts based on a mental distillation of my experiences in teaching physics, primarily at the introductory level, to those whose motivation for taking the course may range from plans to major in it, to idle interest, or as a way to fill out one's course schedule with something that fulfills a general education requirement.

Teaching—and learning—any subject well is not easy; there is no straightforward procedure that can be applied. The more I consider the matter of teaching, the more I realize how little we know about how we learn. In part, I believe that may be due to the fact that learning always occurs within a context or situation that has a history. So it is that educational circumstances are always changing and the paths and directions of educational efforts must change and adapt accordingly. One hallmark of good teaching is honest critical examination that leads to informed modification and adaptation of educational efforts. I will leave it to the reader to judge whether what is written here constitutes an honest critique, but an examination it is, and a reflection and appreciation as well.

THE PECULIAR CHALLENGES OF PHYSICS

In addressing the question of "what works" in teaching—and learning—physics, it seems that early in the discussion one must deal with the legendary reputation of the subject as a difficult one. Indeed, if the course selection behavior of students is considered, physics is a relatively unpopular science as well, in both high school and college. If truth be told, *I* find it difficult. I did when I first began to study the subject and I still find much of it difficult, even after years as a student, as a practicing physicist in industry, and now as a professor.

Let me try to state things regarding its difficulty more precisely. I can pose to myself questions as to the workings of things, but finding answers that I feel are truly insightful and satisfying can take a good deal of time and thought. Mother Nature just does not dish out answers readily; when they arrive, they often do not have quite the form that we expect or anticipate. But I suppose that is part of the attraction, the intrigue, like a murder mystery in which the most innocent-looking person turns out to be the culprit. Would it be more interesting if it were any easier, or its answers more readily obvious?

I do not think it is the challenge of difficulty that makes physics attractive to me, or to other physicists for that matter. No, it is in the answers it provides to questions about how things in the world work, answers that usually demand sustained and enduring curiosity before they reveal themselves but that, once understood, can reveal the workings of laws and principles whose scope of applicability can be breathtaking. It can be like encountering a new tool, unfamiliar in appearance and at first awkward to use, but for which one finds ever more use in tasks that one might have previously thought impossible.

Learning physics requires one to employ particular intellectual approaches and mental efforts, but they must be supported, even driven, by an abiding interest in the how and why of physical occurrences and a tenacity in the pursuit of such questions. It seems that a great determinant in *beginning* to learn physics is whether one has that particularly curious state of mind about physical things that makes one keep asking and trying. This observation is not much help for one trying to teach the subject better, since it reflects the fact that one of the biggest factors in learning is one over which the teacher has little or no control—the prior state of mind of the student.

When describing certain phenomena or processes for the first time to students, I often query them as to where they might have first encountered them. As they scratch their heads wondering, I suggest that it is often simply in playing with toys and I seek ways for students to draw on and reexamine past experiences with physical things so that they can see where the images created and lessons learned from them now deserve a deeper look. It is in these sorts of mundane interactions with physical things that the questions are formed in one's mind. (Of course it has to be the right kind of toy, and computer games do not seem particularly successful at fostering the kind of curiosity I am looking for.)

The common view that the learning of physics is mathematical is incomplete. I find that the most important kind of mathematics that is operative in learning elementary physics is the geometrical. It is true that at almost any level, physics also employs algebra, and trigonometry as well. And to really learn working physics, the kind that can be applied to real problems for which one gets paid for solving, one simply must bring in the tool chest of calculus, and more. And we cannot leave out computers. But for the beginner to grasp the first concepts, it is geometry. The geometric character of physics is unexpected for many new students. Thinking that physics involves calculations ("What formula do I use?"), they do not easily take to seeing the subject as one demanding the construction of pictures in one's head, of imagining the physical arrangements of objects and their interactions. This sort of concept formation forces one to think back and reflect on one's own experiences with *things* and their behavior. Suppose one has not had much—or any—experience with such things and behaviors? As children nowadays seem to spend more of their time on computer games, and less with three-dimensional toys and other mechanical contraptions, such experiential voids are increasingly common. If the examples of physics involve things being pushed or rolled, slid, twirled or tilted or if they involve pulleys, inclines, seesaws and merry-go-rounds, the learning experience gets abstract rather quickly if one's childhood play has not included these things. A decent ability for geometric imagination can compensate somewhat for a lack of experience with physical things, but there has to be enough knowledge of real things to enable one to form mental images of their physical behavior. I have found that it can be useful to poke a bit with questions in order to discern the range of relevant prior experiences of one's students. They are not likely to easily volunteer that they do not know what a tetherball is or that they have no idea of the difference between caliper and drum brakes.

It has been said by others that one of the big challenges in introducing physics to people is to have them confront their own misconceptions about many physical processes. Almost everyone has some sense of not *how* physical things behave under particular conditions, but how they *think* they behave. If this sense is derived from careful and repeated observation made with enough attention and awareness to allow one to recognize both generalities and unique peculiarities in the situations observed, the recollection of these observations can help. But quite often one's recollection is imperfect because the situations of the experiences were either not broad enough or were simply not observed with enough care and attention. In coming to an understanding of basic principles, one often has to *un*learn as one learns the subject, coming to see the limitations or peculiarities of one's recollected experiences. This inherent difficulty at the outset is more than off-putting to many people. It can be frustrating and discouraging. With some students I have found it more than helpful, often downright necessary, to let them experiment in an open-ended fashion in lab with whatever mechanical things might not have been part of their childhood but that exhibit the principles I wish to teach them.

CUSTOMARY AND USUAL PRACTICE

In the last decade or so, controversial discussion over a canon of source books has gone on in many subjects of the liberal arts. Introductory physics courses have for a long time had their own canon, the sequence of topics that have provided the content of the vast majority of introductory courses. This "canon" of sorts is pretty much the same no matter what the composition of the student audience, with probably the major distinguishing characteristic being in the amount and kind of mathematics employed by each, leading to the course descriptors "calculus-based" and "algebra-based." (In fact, in light of what I wrote earlier, both of them have to be geometry-based to get anywhere.) Those who have taught introductory physics can run through the usual arrangement of topics in their dreams: mechanics, electricity and magnetism to start with, and then waves and sound, fluids, temperature and heat, light and optics, wherever they will fit. All of this is followed by "modern physics," making the rest of it sound like medieval science. And within each of these topics are subtopics, like vectors with mechanics, projectiles with free fall, and so on. Associated with each topic are typical problems, often assigned as homework, sometimes done in lecture as examples. One can look at an introductory text fifty years old and see very little change in the topic selection compared to today's books. There are some notable variations, or renovations, but sooner or later the topical progression in introductory courses will all likely include, to one degree or another, the aforementioned topics.

This conventional syllabus structure makes for a conventional pattern of coverage on the part of the professor. It also makes for a conventional pattern of internal expectations. What happens if one does not cover all of the topics? What professor has not anticipated the possible shame that will be theirs if their students, upon progressing to a subsequent course for which the introduction is a prerequisite, show themselves to be ignorant of certain prior topics, an ignorance possibly traceable back to one's own failure to cover it in the introduction? No, every teacher of physics wants to be able to confidently declare (or lie convincingly), "I taught them *that*." Every physics professor has felt on his or her neck the hot breath of the calendar schedule while checking the pace of the course against the table of contents and the number of weeks remaining in the term. One can almost come to feel as if teaching the subject is like trying to get the rest of the lawn mowed before the failing daylight cuts the work short. It is not so bad if it is the only, or the last, physics course the class will be taking, as is usually the case with a class of nonmajors. If they miss a question on the MCAT's (medical college admission test) because it was not covered, it will never get back to you, the teacher. Then there is the method that seems to have been used on me, of covering as many of the chapters in the given volume as one reasonably can, and leave it to the students to cover the rest. After all, you tell yourself, they have been given a good foundation. The next term, you begin with the next volume. Actually, this seemingly reckless approach, in the right circumstances, just might not be as bad as it sounds, as we will see later.

INQUIRY-BASED LEARNING

A major trend in pedagogy is the incorporation into teaching of what are called activity and inquiry-based learning and methods, and physics is no exception. What do these mean and how do they differ from traditional methods? There are a number of variants, but they all might be generally characterized by a replacement of the traditional lecture format with the presentation to the student of situations and problems for their consideration. Often these problems are posed in a lab setting and are presented by and studied with apparatus, hence the "activity." Sometimes the problems are posed on paper, but presented along with certain carefully framed questions the consideration of which is designed to lead the student through "inquiry" to a discovery of the relevant physical principles. The major justification for the use of such methods is the claim that educational research shows, at least for physics, that many students learn almost nothing in a traditional lecture format. Yes, *nothing*. Well, almost nothing. (You can test the extent of this claim in your own teaching simply by asking students questions about a topic following shortly after your lecturing on it, either in the same session or the next.)

I suppose I have exhibited my own implicit realization of this sad fact when I tell my students of the importance of homework, going so far as to tell them that diligent attention to homework will be more important for their understanding of the subject than will be their dutiful class attendance. I try to impress upon my students that those who see no need to do the homework because they have followed well—or think they have—what I covered in lecture have just about signed their own academic death warrants. A major behavioral indicator of likely eventual success in my course, in my experience, is the asking of questions that arise while working on homework problems.

So why lecture at all? For one, it is efficient, handling large numbers of students at a time. Science departments know well how effectively the scheduling and staffing of laboratory sessions torpedoes the improvement of their departmental faculty workload statistics that are compiled by administrators, even though the smaller group size of labs gives hope of more individual attention. Lecture hall methods allow an institution to, at least on paper, do more with less. That is a reason for lectures based on expediency. It is also a relatively efficient way of outlining for students what it is that they must set out to learn on their own. Another reason, perhaps somewhat elitist, for justifying traditional lecture methods is the claim that for the very best or highly self-motivated students, that format is effective. It is not difficult to see that this is likely so. Probably all of us have derived considerable benefit from attending a public lecture on some topic of concern and interest to us, one on which we may have thought and read a bit. Quite aside from our memory of the perhaps famous person speaking, if what was said was lucid and substantive, the lecture may go far to help us along in the development of our own thinking on the subject. On the other hand, a brilliant exposition on a matter that we have never before thought about is often likely to largely evaporate from our minds shortly thereafter.

The practice of activity and inquiry-based methods does sometimes knowingly sacrifice breadth for a certain kind of depth. If students can learn some concepts well, they will presumably become familiar with the habits of mind and the general workings of physics that are necessary to learn other concepts—or so goes the thinking. I believe that the approach has merit, though there is something about the scope and breadth of topics in physics that is illuminating as well. Recall the approach, mentioned earlier, of covering as many chapters as one can and essentially truncating the remainder at term's end. The reason I said that this approach might not be as bad as it sounds is that, under the right circumstances, covering certain topics well can serve as a foundation for the student to continue the study further, individually and somewhat independently. To some extent, all teaching has that character. I do not think there is any universally satisfactory solution to the matter. At times my students have complained about the amount of material to be covered. My response has been understanding, but somewhat unyielding. There is a big difference between high school and a college curriculum, I tell them. The high school program uses a state-mandated syllabus, which, though extensive perhaps, is at least confined within the covers of a handbook of a finite number of pages. For them, high school led to college. But where does college lead them? Answer: to the big and bad, wide and wild world, where no amount of learning or topic coverage will ever be enough. The only guide for the teacher in the face of all of this is to cover as much as one can, but at a pace and in a manner that attempts to maximize learning. Now that certainly clears things up, does it not?

My Epiphany

Before I continue further, I wish to recollect here the circumstances in which I learned what physics is really all about. It was in a high school physics class, which to some might seem the last place where true insight is attained in anything. We had been working on torque problems, part of the standard New York State Regents syllabus for physics at that time. I can still recall vividly the place, the situation, the time of day, the weather, the quality of the sunlight. I was at a classroom blackboard, along with several other classmates, trying to figure out what is to me now an elementary problem involving the positioning of weights on a beam to achieve balance, really nothing more than the principle underlying the situation of several children of differing weights trying to balance a playground seesaw. I stood there at the board, as confused as any student could be.

Up until then I had not been finding physics particularly easy, but I did find it satisfying, motivated by some sort of vague but steady faith that in its study lay the promise of my finding answers to all sorts of questions I had about, simply put, *things*, how *they* worked, how the *world* worked. But on that morning, at the blackboard, I did not seem to be getting any answers to such questions. The problem posed was clear enough, but there I stood, fumbling around with algebraic expressions for the weights and their positions, not having the dimmest idea if any of it was correct.

Presently the teacher came alongside and began to show me how to properly apply the balance equation for the torques. At that moment, like Saul on his way to Damascus, it all became clear to me. I "got" it, seeing clearly how to set up the appropriate balance equation for the force moments. But I also realized at the same time ever so much more. I immediately understood that the algebraic values stood for real entities whose specific values would change from case to case and that the balance equation was set up according to a rule that was applicable generally to all similar situations.

There was more: if one was sure that the rule was correct and properly applicable to the case at hand, one could predict through calculation what the outcome would be. One could, in effect, determine exactly where a child of a certain mass had to sit to balance a seesaw and know with confidence that it would indeed balance. There was no need to use trial and error. No experimentation was needed. I saw how the torque balance rule succinctly described an entire class of situations, a class containing an infinite number of possible situations. Once one truly had confidence in a general expression for relationships, one could use it to predict the outcome. I saw how it was done and I realized that this would be how it would work with other rules applicable to other phenomena and situations as well. Physics was not just a tool; it was a whole machine shop.

WHAT REALLY WORKS

One universal difference I have found—and it is a big one—between virtually all newer activity and inquiry-based approaches versus the traditional ones is that the former all have a more favorable ratio of both teacher and time to student. The implementation of these methods, which involves posing the situation or problem with care, is invariably in an environment where the student gets—or can get—more time and attention, and better targeted as well. Most activity and inquiry-based approaches are done with class groups no larger than a lab setting, which for many schools translates to a maximum of about two dozen students. These approaches often include the use of additional aides, graduate student assistants working with the professor, or multiple teachers.

As I observed earlier, a full implementation of activity and inquiry-based methods sometimes precludes the effort to deal with all of the material that would have been covered with a more traditional teaching format. Depth in a selected smaller set of topics rather than running over as much of the "canon" as possible might have something to be said for it, but I do not think this is the secret of any success here. It is notable to me that what is likely the most significant aspect of methods based on activity and inquiry is simply increased attention to the student, within a situation constructed to get the student to grapple with the topic, rather than listen to the teacher talk about it. It is something that is very similar to what I was afforded on that morning years ago in high school when I "got it." Having been sent to the board along with several others, each of us to work on a particular problem, I was able to have the teacher monitor my own progress. He was able to assist individually and tailor his instruction to the nature and level of my immediate need. At the right moment, standing at my side, taking up exactly at the point where my ignorance and confusion had brought productive effort on my part to a momentary halt, he was able to say, "Here, Larry, let me show you how it works." None of this is likely possible in a large lecture class and, from what I have seen, it more frequently occurs in settings employing activity and inquiry-based methods. I do not know if I ever have been the facilitator for a burst of insight in the mind of any one of my students comparable to what I experienced on that epiphanous morning of mine. I think I have come close a few times, judging by their happy face when they exclaim, "Oh, so *that's* how it works." But to have any of them experience anything like what I did on that high school morning is worth as much effort as one can muster. So the answer to it all is that one does whatever, *whatever*, one thinks will make such experiences more, rather than less, likely.

Whatever my batting average in this regard might be, I have found absolutely no substitute for getting inside a student's head, for assessing whatever level of understanding or competence he or she might be at, for trying to see how they are conceptualizing. Analysis of a student's reasoning process is critical. There may be one right way—or perhaps a few—to do a problem, but there are many ways to be wrong, and students need to know why their thinking is wrong, as much as they need to understand the correct way. Remember what I said earlier about unlearning the subject. People will not give up their misconceptions unless and until they understand how and why they are incorrect. And you do this by whatever means works. Activity and inquiry-based methods seem to hold the promise of offering much of this in the greatest amounts to the greatest numbers, but there is no magic there. Sometimes an office visit will do the trick, a phone call to the teacher while working on a problem, a small-group problem or recitation session, a trial quiz problem checked immediately thereafter by the student. It is very difficult to do this in large group settings. Individual attention at the right moment does appear even more critical when there is a presentation of a topic or problem in a way that invites an inquiry-based approach or guided activities. After listening to a poor lecture, a student can at least turn to the textbook, but giving a lab activity that leaves the student lost seems a good way to head the student toward a truly robust hate for science.

Finding out exactly what our students have learned requires both honesty and effort. What is my reaction when most of the class fails to give the correct solution to an exam question? The analysis of test results that yield such information can be illuminating. For class size of at most two or three dozen, one can perform analysis of individual student responses to long-answer questions to useful effect. For larger classes—and smaller ones as well—tests made in a multiple-choice format can be useful too, if one constructs and selects questions with care and performs success rate analysis of responses. Automated scoring of scan sheets with their associated automated statistical analysis capabilities can take a lot of the drudgery out of such work. Of course this requires us to make something better of things when most of the class has gotten a particular question wrong. Does the difficulty lie with us or with them? I will leave that for the reader to ponder along with the question as to what will you do if you determine that the reasons lie with them.

Other ways of trying to get inside the heads of students? An analyst of business practices once characterized a particular executive method for the workplace as "management by walking around." In the practice, one spends a lot of time out of one's own office chair, talking informally to members of one's work team, sometimes asking questions, but often just listening. Coffee breaks become technical conversations. Chance encounters in the hallway breed the discussion of new ideas. In this way one might better get a sense of the flow and status of the work as well as problems than by formal meetings and interviews. With students in a science course, lab sessions are good places to put this into practice. As I walk around the lab, watching different groups work, I get students to talk about themselves, their prior schooling, their career intentions, and, if I am really lucky, they might even volunteer information about difficulties they are having in physics. At the very least, it is a good way to learn their names. One can see how an inquiry-based course format might make this easier to do. Here again, meaningful exchanges almost always occur one-on-one or among the lab group of three or four students. And once the session size exceeds about eighteen, it becomes very difficult to do without running oneself ragged.

For each and every student, one should never give up hope and yet never rest on success. Beyond my observation that the quality of student performance early on in my course is quite often a good indicator of eventual outcome, there have been a number of cases when my own private predications have shown themselves spectacularly wrong—the old nature versus nurture argument in a new setting. In any event, though it may be that we have no control over the prior experience of the student, it nevertheless seems essential to meet the student as close as possible to the point at which such prior experience has brought him or her. In teaching a class of a diverse background, I try to make it clear at the outset what is the cluster of topical prerequisites that I am assuming, and we all have to make some. If my instructional approach is to assume that the student has had a high school physics course, I state so clearly, and conversely. In a few cases, this leads to a course withdrawal on the student's part; however, in most cases, it amounts to an advisory that the student must be aware that there may be some places in the course where it will seem that something is missing. The burden will be on the student to ask questions. Success in this regard ultimately depends on convincing the student that it is better to ask a hundred questions that prove superfluous than to have one important and necessary question go unasked. But how to get a student to abandon reserve in that regard? The only answer I can offer is anything that works. I have taken to passing out office visit coupons, which must be redeemed within a set number of days. Office visits such as these made under mild duress usually have students ask questions about the subject or reveal useful information about their backgrounds that would otherwise go undiscovered.

Anything that goads students to consider homework problems helps. The learning that takes place in lecture and lab pales in significance to that acquired by working on homework problems. The real goal of homework is to get the student to exercise thoughtful and somewhat independent reflection on the topic, without which there will be no concept formation occurring in their own heads. Collecting homework regularly and reviewing it at least for evidence of respectable attention, rather than for complete correctness of response, seems to help, but students usually heed the assignment of homework more when they also get some sort of numerical indicator of quality. Brief quizzes on chapter readings and requiring students to pose a question do not seem to hurt either. Some prior guidance seems wise as they begin to read a new chapter in a physics text. This stuff is *not* easy and it helps if I give them guidelines as to what to spend most of their effort on and what to omit, for one can never get it all in a first reading. It does not seem to hurt to tell them that in many respects introductory physics is far harder than more advanced levels of the subject. If it took the human race more than a thousand years for Galileo and Newton to arrive on the scene and improve upon Aristotle's ideas about motion, they should not feel too bad if it takes them more than a few days to retrace those steps.

THE USE OF TECHNOLOGY

As a member of the community of scientists whose kind gave the world the computer, I would like to offer a few words on the employment of technology in the classroom. First, people often apply the term "technology" here in a way that pains me. While the word usually refers to the presence of any microprocessor-based machine in the classroom, the piece of polished slate we call a blackboard is "technology," as is the white markerboard that is its latter day replacement. For that matter, so is the use of 5 mil plastic sheet to protect classroom valuables (like computers) from rain through a leaky roof. To my mind, technology is not computers in a classroom, nor is it an image projector, a camera, or even an overhead transparency projector. Educational technologies are those products of engineering that we employ to help us accomplish our teaching tasks more effectively. If that happens to mean computers, and everything that goes with them, then all is well.

Whatever implementation of technology is brought to the classroom ought to be the result of the informed choice of the teacher, made in order to assist in the accomplishment of certain teaching tasks and the attainment of certain educational objectives. You might say, "But of course, that is what all that hardware is there for." I would say that is how it is supposed to be, but that these things are often done backwards, with technology products provided before a decent amount of thought as to how they are to be used. I say that the selection of particular hardware ought to be made only after the teacher has attempted to describe what it is that he or she is trying to do instruction-wise, *independent of considerations of particular hardware*. Then, with the description of those instructional goals in mind, a person knowledgeable about instructional technology can assist in the selection of appropriate hardware. Far too often, certain hardware sets are installed in classrooms seemingly driven by an educational juggernaut. Whether it is a big screen at the front of the room or a laptop for every student, the thinking seems to be that, if we do not also have it, then the technological bandwagon will leave us behind. All right, I like the big screen idea a lot more than the laptop thing, but I am speaking with *my* teaching needs in mind, not *yours*. Having said all that, the following are ways in which I use or hope to use "technology" to good advantage. Remember, I am a physicist, for the most part an experimental and industrial one at that, and I count on technology as a thoroughly necessary tool.

Assignment of homework has always been a challenge for me. I have never, ever, been able to stay on a lesson plan. All I have to do is ask, "Any questions?" and my attempt to deal with them will invariably lead me off the plan. How do I tailor assignments to the progress and immediate needs of the class? Enter technology! What I frequently now do is hold off on the assignment of homework until I have had time to go back to my office and reflect on things a bit. Then I use class list email or a web-based class management product to send out the homework, now tailored to that day's classroom happenings, adding to or deleting from my initial homework plan as I see fit. This is also a great channel for giving students chapter-reading guidelines.

Another capability afforded by available technology that I have found useful, through the use of a document camera and a projector, is the immediate presentation to the entire class of a particular student's written work. This capability offers immense promise. Think of how absurd it would be if, when we held a classroom discussion, we had each participant first record their words and then play them back for the class. How awkward and pointless. Yet this is sort of the thing we must resort to when we have a student put his or her work on the board for viewing by the whole class. First they do the work; then, while we all wait, they put the work on the board for the rest of us to see. With a document camera, or better, with two of them, one can immediately display student paperwork to the entire class, then critique, compare, and contrast it with other students' efforts. Such a capability is particularly useful in physics where the analysis of problems might require the construction of certain diagrams or other pictorial representations.

In the physics lab, the use of computer-based sensors and data-processing routines in the data collection and analysis is commonplace, as are spreadsheets and graphing programs. Simulation and demonstration software packages are readily available. Some course programs make these tools the centerpiece of instructional pathways. Such software tools offer much promise, but most of them appear to me to assume an ability on the part of the student to imagine, to conceptualize, the workings of physical things. Where experience with real physical objects is lacking, the use of the program runs the risk of degenerating into a kind of computer game. I do believe that computer simulations offer some significant promise because, provided that students have some amount of experience with manipulation of real objects, simulations will allow cyberstudy of a wider range of varied circumstances than could be achieved with concrete objects and situations. Because they allow initial conditions to be set by the learner, computer simulations enable one to readily explore the implications and results of one's own questions and hunches.

To What Does It All Lead?

Like most teachers and professors in physics, I have taught all sorts of audiences. There are those who need to learn the principles and the analytical methods of the discipline in order to put them to use in their chosen career. Engineers, applied mathematicians, some chemists, geologists and biologists, and physicists themselves constitute this group. Others will need some understanding of how physical principles enable or bind together the workings of certain circumstances. This group might include everyone from those dealing with factory and industrial processes to workers in health services, including physical therapists, nurses, and many doctors. There are those who might want to know how the principles of physics are manifest in such everyday things as energy production and transport, weather, and communications. And there are those who want to know about black holes, anti-matter, artificial life and intelligence, and other such imponderables.

To all of these groups there is something I hope to convey that is well captured by the title of an autobiography by the physicist John Wheeler, *At Home in the Universe*. What a wonderful image the title conveys! Throughout history, humankind has feared the appearance of certain natural events, ascribing them to supernatural evil until we learned enough meteorology and geology to convince (some of) us otherwise. We feared the ocean until the knowledge of the geometry of a round earth, of the stars and celestial navigation, and of terrestrial magnetism and the behavior of lodestones allowed us to literally find our way around the world. After the development of a rudimentary ability in metallurgy that was solely empirical, we fumbled around with alchemy, but with the eventual discovery of the periodic table we made ordered, patterned sense of the seeming jigsaw puzzle of chemicals around us. We wondered what makes living things so, and observed that certain things "ran in families," but had no real idea why until we found a good part of the answer in the structure of DNA. We discovered these things because in large measure we found answers to some of the questions physicists ask.

If we are to navigate this earth and study the universe, rather than just wander through it like someone lost in the forest, if we are to find any answer as to the why of the blueness of the sky or the twinkle of a star, it will be because of the physics we learn and understand. If in teaching the subject I can cultivate in students a sense of the comfort and security and satisfaction that can be the outcome of such knowledge, it will be time well spent.

I think of a day years ago when I was many feet up on the side of a rock face in the Grand Tetons. My toes and one hand were clinging to the rock while my remaining free hand was groping around, here, there, for a hold. I looked up and higher, for anything to grab, and noted reflexively that the sun was in my eyes. The leader, who sat atop and to whom I was roped (I am too cautious a person to have put myself into such a predicament alone), said, "Larry, the sun is trying to tell you something." Ah yes. Moving my hand away and further to one side, away from the glare of the sun, out of sight but just above and over, was the "bucket," a hold so secure that it made everything thereon an easy scramble to the top.

Physics is like that: sometimes a seeming dead-end path, with nothing to grip, nothing to suggest a way further. Natural signals, like the sunlight in one's eyes, seem to frustrate more than guide. It might even seem impossible. But then, a bit more exploration, sometimes in places that do not seem to be promising, and a path, or an answer, materializes. The satisfaction of learning a bit more about how the world works is as satisfying to me as was that successful climb up a rock face, an ascent that I might have previously never dared. Just as on that day my persistence rewarded me with a successful climb over warm, sunlit rock, today and tomorrow I hope to impart in students my sense of confidence that persistent effort, whether in the lab or with paper and pencil, will lead them to satisfying answers to questions about "how it works that way." As I was on that day at home on the rock, I hope an understanding of physics can make them feel at home in the universe.

REFERENCE

Wheeler, John Archibald. *At Home in the Universe.* Woodbury, NY: AIP Press, 1994.

13

Psi Fi: Learning Psychology Through Active Engagement in Science Fiction

William E. Herman
Psychology

> I have lost interest in being a teacher....I am only interested in being a learner.
> —Carl R. Rogers

Many, perhaps most, professors joined the academic ranks in order to maintain the momentum of intellectual stimulation nurtured in graduate school and to make a positive difference in the lives of students and society. At a fundamental level, such goals focus on the exploration, creation, advancement, maintenance, critical assessment, and reality testing of knowledge. The purpose of this chapter is to share in considerable depth and detail how my teaching of psychology dovetailed in an undergraduate course with a personal interest in science fiction.

PERSONAL BELIEFS ABOUT LEARNING AND TEACHING

After over a quarter of a century of college/university teaching experience at several institutions, I have formulated a personal credo about teaching and learning. It is crucial for readers to understand something about my philosophy, theoretical bias, and instructional approach at the a priori level. This chapter will proceed deductively and conclude with an explanation of how I have chosen to employ science fiction in the teaching of psychology.

I need to confess that much of what follows grows out of my personal experience with thousands of students and graduate studies at two midwestern institutions. These events helped me construct a coherent philosophical and theoretical basis for my teaching. When searching for answers to instructional problems, I carefully examine a wide variety of theoretical viewpoints, but somehow continue to return to the following two arenas for inspiration: (1) the set of ideals outlined in humanistic psychology by Carl R. Rogers, Abraham Maslow, Howard Kirschenbaum, and many others, and (2) the constructivist approach to teaching and learning currently so popular that rests on the ideas of John Dewey, Jean Piaget, and Lev Vygotsky. The integration of these seemingly disparate viewpoints is pragmatically possible. Herman and Gwaltney (1999) outlined the connections between humanistic psychology and cognitive psychology and how six principles might promote the future construction of knowledge.

Those familiar with teaching and learning theory will recognize these ideas are hardly new. In fact, it is downright difficult, if not impossible, to formulate a new approach to teaching and learning that does not in some crucial ways reflect the influence of these viewpoints. What is not only possible, but essential, is to discover a way to synthetically weave the best ideas together to form a learning tapestry capable of meeting current educational objectives such as more deeply involving more students, and helping students see the practical application of knowledge.

EDUCATIONAL CREDO

Here are some of the things I have learned.

Unfortunately, much of what passes for teaching and learning is the memorization of factual information of questionable importance (at least to many learners and even some teachers) and the regurgitation of such facts on paper. In stark contrast, I am much more interested in teaching that promotes personal learning among students and results in conceptual change and the application of ideas, theories, and research findings. Learners and teachers must openly share why certain ideas are more useful than others. When the value and usefulness of ideas are explored, I also actively become involved as a learner and discard the sometimes-comforting role of the sole intellectual authority in the class-room. The need to learn factual information best emerges after this process due to improvement in the motivation to learn.

Learning is a cooperative venture where trust, risk taking, healthy relationships, and the proper interpersonal chemistry can, in the Gestalt tradition, result in an eventual outcome that is greater than the unitary sum of the collective contributions. It takes courage to risk breaking down the formidable barriers that traditionally divide students and teachers. It involves viewing traditional knowledge—that at times assumes sacred status—from different vantage points and seeking good questions as well as excellent answers. As my mentor, Tom Gwaltney, taught me decades ago, serendipitous meanderings of the mind can lead to unpredictable and productive outcomes.

Learning is best accomplished when ideas, concepts, and terms are organized into meaningful categories and relationships are clarified. Human memory skills such as recall, retrieval, and recognition are likely to be enhanced when such a complex structure of knowledge is in place. Successful learners strive to learn how knowledge in a field was arrived at and is currently best organized, and relate new knowledge to already existing knowledge.

As a facilitator of learning, I see myself in the role of assisting students and also carrying on my own construction and deconstruction of knowledge, organization of knowledge (e.g., in the realm of similarities and differences between ideas), application of knowledge to practical and real-life situations, and critical evaluation of ideas and proposed solutions to problems. I have been constantly reminded during my teaching that I cannot force another human being to learn. Learners must make significant contributions to this learning process, but teachers can contribute in a necessary way also. Substantial learning occurs as a result of the ideal instructional interaction, whereby neither student nor teacher can claim to be a more significant contributor to learning. A teacher can become the "guide from the side," a collaborative learner, rather than just the "sage on the stage." I have the professional responsibility to challenge students by proposing ideas and solutions they might not have considered, but, in the end, it is the individual student who must determine if my contributions or their own ideas are worthy and valuable. I frequently find that I need to more deeply listen to my students.

Although the past, present, and future all can be crucial factors in the learning process, gigantic leaps forward in learning seem to take place when learners are fully present in the moment and discover personal meaning. The fact that learning is not always efficient cannot be over-stated. The change models that promote conceptual mental change and personal meaning seem best suited for one-to-one and small group experiences (perhaps ten to twelve students is an ideal upper limit). It is unrealistic to expect that even a majority of perhaps 100 or more students seated in a large lecture hall will experience the type of personal learning of which I am speaking.

A Thought Experiment

I started thinking about offering a new course in psychology by asking myself the following question: "Where do we allow ourselves as professors and our students to dream and consider what the future might be like?" Follow-up questions quickly leaped into my dialectical consciousness such as: "Wouldn't the best and brightest students on campus, who are likely destined to be future leaders in society, have unique viewpoints on such a topic?" and "Doesn't the genre of science fiction already offer excellent literary examples of how scientific thinking has been logically extended to futuristic settings?"

It was this form of thinking (a thought experiment) that led me to reminisce about how my own pre-teenage reading of science fiction might have in a subtle manner encouraged me to become an educational psychologist. Such thinking also forced me to remember reading B. F. Skinner's *Walden Two*. I found this Utopian novel fascinating, challenging, and disturbing all at the same time and for different reasons. Surely, I thought, there must be many other works of social science fiction that could be employed in a course that examined the intersections of psychology and other social sciences with science fiction. Some of my best and brightest students had already admitted they were sci-fi fans. My guess was that I had found a market niche for such a course.

My first task was to organize my ideas and search for resources that could accomplish the broad goal of exploring psychological or social science fiction. Fortunately, these resources were easy to find. Asimov (1971) defined social science fiction as "that branch of literature which is concerned with the impact of scientific advance upon human beings" (272). This broad and inclusive definition was inviting. Soon I discovered that many other psychologists and educators also had seen the potential of employing science fiction as a vehicle for learning decades earlier. The following books by their very titles documented this fact: *Introductory Psychology Through Science Fiction*

(Katz, Warrick, and Greenberg, 1974), *Psychology in the Wry* (Baker, 1963), and *School and Society Through Science Fiction* (Olander, Greenberg, and Warrick, 1974). Other authors also have discovered the potential film brings to the teaching of psychology in such books as: *Jungian Reflections Within the Cinema: A Psychological Analysis of Sci-Fi and Fantasy Archetypes* (Iaccino, 1998) and *Movies & Mental Illness: Using Films to Understand Psychopathology* (Wedding and Boyd, 1999).

THE COURSE EXPERIMENT

As I started to write the proposal to offer the course as part of the campus-wide Honors Program, I decided to build the syllabus for the Honors Council to review in order to gain a more complete picture of this potential course offering. The following course description was generated:

> This course will explore the intersection of the field of psychology and social science fiction. The rich portrayal of psychological, sociological, anthropological, political, historical, and other social science themes in science fiction will serve as a unique vantage point to understand the impact of science upon literature and film and what it means to be human in a social setting.

> *Prerequisite:*

> Admission to the SUNY Potsdam Honors Program and completion of an introduction to a social science discipline (e. g., PSYC-100 Introduction to Psychology, SOCI-101 Introduction to Sociology, ANTC-102 Introduction to Cultural Anthropology, etc.) or permission of the instructor.

Since the course proposal had to be eventually reviewed formally by the General Education Committee to be officially designated for Social Analysis (SA) credit, particular attention needed to be paid to the course objectives. Most institutions have some sort of general education program guidelines that could be an excellent resource in developing any new course. The following course objectives were in the approved version of the proposal:

> 1. Students will study how psychologists and other social scientists systematically investigate human behavior,

human social interactions and relationships, and contemporary social institutions.

2. Students will learn how the historical, theoretical, and philosophical ideas in psychology have resulted in the following contemporary psychological viewpoints: psychoanalysis, behavioristic, humanistic, and cognitive.

3. Students will explore the intersection of psychology as a social science and fiction writing in the humanities that offers an imaginative method of approaching human dilemmas, pursuing truth, disseminating ideas, and seeking societal change.

4. Students will learn that psychologists draw heavily on a variety of quantitative and qualitative methodologies such as empirical data collection, clinical records, case studies, ethnographic techniques, interviews, self-report, and other tools to interpret and analyze human interaction in a social context.

5. Students will observe that the critical analysis of social science fiction can serve as a catalyst for understanding human behavior and social issues from various theoretical viewpoints in psychology and other social science disciplines.

6. Students will discover how fiction that incorporates psychological viewpoints allows for a deeper understanding of the following social issues: human learning, gender identity, gender roles, free will, societal control, freedom to learn, and human sexuality.

7. Students will understand how social science fiction can offer fresh vantage points for making personal and public policy decisions.

Enrollment during the first semester was only four students, but one year later at the next time the course was offered enrollment swelled to twelve students. A specialized course like this needs to be well publicized and students in the course were an excellent recruitment device. They essentially recruited their friends and significant others who had an interest in sci fi and psychology. The occasional film nights when students from the class and any other interested person on campus were invited proved to advance the public relations element of the course offering.

The required reading list for the course included three paperback books in psychology designed to provide an overview and grounding in the field of psychology as a social science. These three books

(Brannigan and Merrens, 1993, 1995; Nye, 1998) were considered highly engaging for students to read, demonstrated the diverse methods of investigation employed by psychologists, and depicted the connectedness of psychology to other social science and natural science disciplines such as sociology, biology, anthropology, politics, history, and so on. During the third round of teaching this course, the two books (Brannigan and Merrens, 1993, 1995) were replaced by the book: *Psychologists Defying the Crowd: Stories of Those Who Battled the Establishment and Won* (Sternberg, 2002). This change was in part due to one of the original books going out of print, but it also offered advantages in fewer required books for purchase, less reading for students, and more stories about contemporary psychologists.

I also used a well-researched teaching strategy that helped students organize psychological knowledge into four current viewpoints (psychoanalytic, behavioristic, humanistic, and cognitive) as we moved through the course (Herman, 1998, 2001). Although most students who registered for the class had a solid background in psychology (most were psychology majors), I made every attempt to cover basic psychological content in the first two weeks for those in the course who were not psychology majors.

Although many excellent novels could have been selected for students to read, the need to reflect diversity of focus and limited class time resulted in the following required reading choices: *Walden Two* (Skinner, 1948), *Fahrenheit 451* (Bradbury, 1996), and *The Left Hand of Darkness* (Le Guin, 1996). Other books that might be used in future semesters include: *Brave New World* (Huxley, 1946), *1984* (Orwell, 1949), and *A Clockwork Orange* (Burgess, 1967).

Equally challenging was the selection of short stories for students to read in the course from the wide array of literary works that deal with ideas and issues that were a focus of the course. The following stories are currently on a list that I have used in the past or plan to use in the future (see the reference list for sources):

Author	Short Story
Octavia Butler (1996)	"Bloodchild"
David A. Kyle (1968)	"Deadlier Specie"
James V. McConnell (1957)	"Learning Theory"
James V. McConnell (1953)	"Life Sentence"
T. Coraghessan Boyle (1998)	"Modern Love"
Donald Keys (1982)	"Rewiring the Human Being: A Feasibility Study"
Horace Miner (1956)	"Body Ritual Among the Nacirema"
Lois Gould (1992)	"X: A Fabulous Child's Story"
Roy Baumeister and Kathleen Vohs (2003)	"Sobriety Epidemic Endangers Nation's Well-being"

The following film sources are also on a constantly growing list of classroom resources that has either been used or might be in the future:

> *Dr. Jekyll and Mr. Hyde* (1941—colorized in 1998)
> *Fahrenheit 451* (1966)
> *Forbidden Planet* (1956)
> *Planet of the Apes* (1968)
> *Mary Shelley's Frankenstein* (1994)
> *Star Trek the Next Generation Episode: "Phantasms"* (1994)
> *Twilight Zone* television series episodes
> *Amazing Stories* television series episodes

Students in the class during the fall semester of 2001 were able to take advantage of a fortuitous event: the art exhibit entitled UFO Show, on campus at the Gibson Art Gallery. This traveling exhibit was organized by Illinois State University and became an unanticipated point of discussion during the class. I am always searching for local community and campus events that might be connected to our topics when the course is taught each fall.

Three other unique aspects of the course deserve to be noted here. It might even be argued that the following elements were essential in making this class a success.

First, I had access to David A. Kyle: a science fiction historian, writer, illustrator, publisher, and editor in the local community. David is an octogenarian and noted authority in the field as evidenced by his rich background and publications, which include *A Pictorial History of Science Fiction* (Kyle, 1976) and *The Illustrated Book of Science Fiction Ideas and Dreams* (Kyle, 1977). David visited class several times during the semester when he watched films with us, outlined the history of science fiction, and talked about personal encounters with Ray Bradbury, Arthur C. Clarke, Isaac Asimov, Damon Knight, Stanley Kubrick, and others. He also helped students think about storytelling and the development of characters within the limitations of a short story.

Second, each student wrote a short social science fiction story of approximately 2,000 words to gain a deeper appreciation of science fiction. As the course instructor, I read a section of my own unfinished manuscript in this genre. David Kyle agreed to read each student's story, if they desired, and offer editorial feedback. It should to be noted that a few students explicitly decided not to have David read their stories. This request was always honored and such a student decision did not influence the instructor's grading of this assignment.

The goal was not to produce a publishable science fiction story, but rather to learn by doing after reading considerably in the field and grasping the complexities of using one's creative imagination and polishing one's writing and storytelling skills. The most valuable lesson learned by the majority of the students included how much work (thought, revision, and rewriting) and time went into such a short story. It seemed obvious that many students walked away from the class with a deeper respect for the process of fiction writing and the authors who devote their lives to the pursuit of creating literary works.

Third, everyone in the class (including David Kyle and myself) worked on an artistic project throughout the semester that celebrated psychology, the social sciences, and science fiction. Visual images were collected during the semester and glued onto one-inch foam-board tiles to create a "Psi Fi" mosaic image. Support for the project was easily obtained from the president, provost, deans, department chairs, faculty members, and other invited guests who each completed individual mosaic tiles that were included in the finished product. Students in the class seemed impressed that so many prominent people on campus supported our project by contributing mosaic tiles.

A total of 320 mosaic tiles made up the 16 X 20 inch framed work of art that was unveiled near the end of the semester and donated to the Department of Psychology where it is permanently on public display. All class participants were later given a photocopied reproduction of the original mosaic suitable for framing as an item of course memorabilia.

The PSI FI motif represented in the mosaic served at the phonetic level to remind participants and viewers that we were representing science fiction or sci-fi in the more colloquial form. The exchange of the word psi for sci might need some further explanation. As every well-schooled student of psychology knows, the letter psi in the Greek alphabet is also the official designation for the field of psychology. Many psychological professional organizations have embedded the written form of this Greek letter (ψ) into their logos.

It is especially difficult to evaluate the impact of this artistic element of the course due to the inherent subjective nature of artistic endeavors. It is easy to affirm that it was a popular activity, but what did students actually learn from creating this mosaic? Class time was designated for each student to talk about the tiles they created and how these visual and/or written messages reflected what they had learned in the class. Obviously, there was not enough time for every student to talk about every tile generated, but enough discussion was allowed so that I felt assured that students had made connections that were not likely to have been made at the beginning of the course. The meanings embedded in the mosaic tiles in some cases were obvious and function at a public level, while other meanings were more personal and remained at the private level. Such dual attributional expressions of personal meaning and public awareness are often reflected in art.

As a final note, I wish to acknowledge that other class guests (in addition to David Kyle) gave generously of their time by sharing their expertise with my students and encouraging us as the mosaic was being created. For example, Dr. Debra S. Pate, a colleague on campus, came to discuss feminism and the Le Guin book. When we tackled a *Star Trek* episode dealing with the schizoid personality disorder, a colleague, Dr. Richard Williams, visited class to discuss clinical disorders and the *Diagnostic and Statistical Manual of Mental Disorders IV* (APA, 1994).

Course Assessment and Outcomes

Any reputable course or project must be evaluated. Formative and summative evaluation provided essential benchmarks to assess the success of the course (see Bloom, Hastings, and Madaus, 1971). The formative elements took place before and during the instructional phase of the course. Personal reflection and the application for approval from the Honors Program and the General Education Program served as major checkpoints. The *SUNY Potsdam General Education Faculty Manual: Defining Criteria for Course Designation Guidelines* included guidance on the design of course objectives and the linkage of assessment strategies to such objectives. At the semester midpoint, I devoted three hours to a careful self-examination of where we were in the course and where we were headed. Detailed notes were taken for later use in modifying the course in future semesters. Minor changes were made in sequencing of films and timing of an essay exam during the latter half of the semester as a result of this formative evaluation.

The summative evaluation strategy relied primarily on the Student Evaluation of Instruction Form provided by the SUNY Potsdam Honors Program. In general, the anonymous ratings and comments from the sixteen students over two semesters were extremely positive. A sample of comments are listed below:

> "It was fun as well as educational."
> "A lot of reading, but I know it was necessary."
> "The discussions allowed for a variety of viewpoints to be presented."

"It opened my eyes to the field of science fiction."
"I loved all of the novels—very appropriate."
"This was a very open class."
"High emphasis upon discussion!"
"We made a mosaic! All students should have this opportunity!
"We even had the opportunity to create our own science fiction
    story and meet David Kyle—a sci fi author! Creating the
    mosaic was the most fun!"
"Lots of discussion. Very interactive class with movies and
    Twilight Zone episodes to see ideas."
"I liked seeing the theories depicted in movies and television
    programs. I was able to see these shows in a new light."
"A lot of times you would miss something important, but
    someone else in class would catch it and mention it in
    the discussions."
"During the class discussions, everyone was willing to participate
    so I was able to listen to many different points of view."
"It was fun and I learned so much about applying psychological
    principles to daily life."

SOLICITED STUDENT EVALUATION (AT THE AUTHOR'S INVITATION)

The Psychology and Science Fiction course was an amazing learning opportunity. It combined elements of psychology and science
fiction, as well as the natural sciences, social sciences, and the
humanities. I feel that this is one reason that it worked so well.
This course also integrated these various elements and allowed for
creativity. As a class, we read several science fiction novels and
short stories, created a mosaic, analyzed Twilight Zone and Star
Trek episodes and films, designed our own science fiction story,
visited a UFO exhibit at the Gibson Gallery on campus, and even
had the wonderful experience of meeting and working with local
science fiction author David Kyle. These are definitely not aspects
of an ordinary college class. The small class size (only 4 students)
allowed for in-depth discussions and each student became an
important contributor. We all learned to work together as a team,
especially when creating the mosaic. The essay exams allowed us to
express what we knew about a topic in great detail, thus encouraging more higher-ordered divergent thinking. Overall, I would have
to say the class worked because it was a fun and interesting way of
learning. I am happy to have had this unique experience.
                                                        —Stacey Pennock

Suggestions for improving the course included using other science
fiction titles and having easier access to the short stories. A couple of

students felt that the reading requirements were a bit too heavy. The general consensus was that the course was based on a good idea, well planned, sufficiently interactive, and effectively delivered.

Why did it work? After some reflection, my analysis is that the course was successful due to a complex interplay of the following key elements:

1. *Interdisciplinary Focus*: This course examined science fiction for key issues related to psychology and other disciplines such as sociology, cultural anthropology, history, political science, biology, and so on.
2. *Experiential Style*: In addition to students experiencing a special genre of literature, class sessions were focused upon viewing and analyzing films. Visitors who could directly contribute to the course objectives (e.g., writing a sci-fi story) and guests helping to create the mosaic maximized involvement in the class.
3. *Seminar Format*: It would seem that the small class size of a dozen students one semester was optimal in building trust, establishing cohesiveness, and promoting a variety of personal viewpoints based on past experiences.
4. *Existential Questions*: This course explored several deep philosophical issues such as: What are the practical benefits and limitations of free will and cultural control devices? How does gender guide and limit our human existence? What does it mean to be human? and Do rewards and punishments always encourage learning?
5. *Application of Structured Knowledge*: Students were able to properly identify psychological and social science themes in literary works and films.
6. *Effective Use of Community Resources*: The guests such as David Kyle, Dr. Debra Pate, and Dr. Richard Williams who could offer unique contributions to meeting the objectives also seemed critical to the course. The involvement of many campus participants in the mosaic created a unifying spirit of involvement in the art project.
7. *Legacy Issues*: The mosaic functions as a historical artifact of the accomplishments of the semester and can be used to ignite future student interest in such a course.

APPLICATION ACROSS DISCIPLINES

My belief is that these issues and other course preparation strategies mentioned earlier could be adapted for application to teaching in other content areas. Since most campuses have General Education and Honors Programs, it is recommended that course designers search for ways to connect their curriculum development with existing guidelines on and off campus. Locating areas of highly intensive interest on the part of capable students seems to be a critical first step. When you have something worthwhile to offer students it becomes crucial to "get the word out" and market the course to interested students. Although this course was targeted primarily to honors students who might already be more prone to have sci-fi interests, the strategy of selectively targeting student populations and getting students to share their excitement about learning in such environments would seem to cross over disciplinary boundaries.

CONCLUSION

Since the design of the course and the experiment of teaching such a successful course stems from my long-time interest in science fiction, this was an invigorating and intellectually stimulating experience. The opportunity to interact with bright students who share some of my interests in psychology, the social sciences, and science fiction offers a reminder of exactly why I decided to enter the professoriate.

It is difficult to place into words how it feels to lead capable students in the exploration of issues related to how social science fiction can help us better understand human existence. I found that some of the student ideas expressed in class clashed with my own. This forced me to think more deeply about my own ideas. One semester, at a student's passionate request, I read a paperback sci fi novel that I know I would never have read had it not been for the enthusiasm of this student. As the opening quotation from Carl R. Rogers (1969) suggests, I also have lost interest in becoming a traditional teacher, since it is more properly the learning experience that strikes a chord and resonates nearest the core of what education should be all about.

REFERENCES

American Psychiatric Association. *Diagnostic and Statistical Manual of Mental Disorders*, 4th ed. Washington, DC: Author, 1994.

Asimov, I. "Social Science Fiction." In D. Allen, Ed., *Science Fiction and the Future*, pp. 263–290. New York: Harcourt Brace Jovanovich, 1971.

Baker, R. A. *Psychology in the Wry.* Princeton, NJ: Van Nostrand, 1963.

Baumeister, R. F., and K. D. Vohs. "Sobriety Epidemic Endangers Nation's Well-being." *American Psychological Society Observer* 16 no. 4 (2003): 13–14.

Bloom, B. S., J. T. Hastings, and G. F. Madaus. *Handbook on Formative and Summative Evaluation of Student Learning.* New York: McGraw-Hill, 1971.

Boyle, T. C. *T. C. Boyle Stories.* New York: Viking, 1998.

Bradbury, R. *Fahrenheit 451.* New York: Ballantine, 1996.

Brannigan, G. G., and M. R. Merrens. *The Undaunted Psychologist: Adventures in Research.* New York: McGraw-Hill, 1993.

Brannigan, G. G., and M. R. Merrens. *The Social Psychologists: Research Adventures.* New York: McGraw Hill, 1995.

Burgess, A. *A Clockwork Orange.* New York: Norton, 1967.

Butler, O. E. *Bloodchild and Other Stories.* New York: Seven Stories, 1996.

Gould, L. "X: A Fabulous Child's Story." In J. A. Kourany, J. P. Sterba, and Tong, R., Eds. *Feminist Philosophies: Problems, Theories, and Applications.* Englewood Cliffs, NJ: Prentice-Hall, 1992.

Herman, W. E. *Helping Students Organize Psychological Knowledge.* Poster presented at the Annual Meeting of the American Psychological Society 5th Institute on the Teaching of Psychology, Washington, DC, May 1998 (ERIC Reproduction Service No. ED420636).

Herman, W. E. *Student Perceptions of Psychological Content as a Predictor of Classroom Success.* Paper presented at the Annual Meeting of the American Psychological Society 8th Institute on the Teaching of Psychology, Toronto, Ontario, Canada, June 2001 (ERIC Document Reproduction Service No. ED454761).

Herman, W. E., and T. M. Gwaltney. *Human Relationships That Nurture and Advance the Construction of Knowledge.* Paper presented at the Annual Meeting of the American Educational Research Association, Montréal, Québec, Canada, April 1999 (ERIC Document Reproduction Service No. ED434871).

Huxley, A. *Brave New World.* New York: Harper, 1946.

Iaccino, J. F. *Jungian Reflections Within the Cinema: A Psychological Analysis of Sci-Fi and Fantasy Archetypes.* Westport, CT: Praeger, 1998.

Katz, H. A., P. Warrick, and M. H. Greenberg. *Introductory Psychology Through Science Fiction.* Chicago: Rand McNally, 1974.

Keys, D. "Rewiring the Human Being: A Feasibility Study." *Journal of Humanistic Psychology* 22 no. 4 (1982): 71–83.

Kyle, D. A. "Deadlier Specie." *If: Science Fiction Worlds of Tomorrow* 18 no. 3 (1968): 69–75.

Kyle, D. A. *A Pictorial History of Science Fiction.* Middlesex, England: Hamlyn, 1976.

Kyle, D. A. *The Illustrated Book of Science Fiction Ideas and Dreams.* Middlesex, England: Hamlyn, 1977.

Le Guin, U. *The Left Hand of Darkness.* New York: Walker, 1996.

McConnell, J. V. "Life Sentence." *Galaxy* 5 no. 4 (1953): 37–49.

McConnell, J. V. "Learning Theory." *If—Worlds of Science Fiction* 7 (1957): 66–81.

Miner, H. "Body Ritual of the Nacirema." *American Anthropologist* 58 no. 3 (1956): 503–507.

Nye, R. D. *Three Psychologies: Perspectives from Freud, Skinner, and Rogers,* 6th ed. Monterey, CA: Brooks Cole, 1998.

Olander, J. D., M. H. Greenberg, and P. Warrick, *School and Society Through Science Fiction.* Chicago: Rand McNally, 1974.

Orwell, G. *1984.* New York: Harcourt, Brace, 1949.

Rogers, C. R. *Freedom to Learn.* Columbus, OH: Charles E. Merrill, 1969.

Skinner, B. F. *Walden Two.* New York: Macmillan, 1948.

Sternberg, R. J., Ed. *Psychologists Defying the Crowd: Stories of Those Who Battled the Establishment and Won.* Washington, DC: American Psychological Association, 2002.

Wedding, D., and M. A. Boyd. *Movies & Mental Illness: Using Films to Understand Psychopathology.* Boston: McGraw-Hill, 1999.

14

Putting Action in Theory: A Liberating Experiential Education

Peg Wesselink
Politics

At the small, rural, public, liberal arts school at which I teach, most of our students have traveled little and are first-generation college attendees. Since going off to college is often their first experience away from home, they enter the institution with emotional and social issues to untangle, and neither high school nor home life have imbued them with a burning desire to learn. Studying often becomes a sidebar to making friends, going to parties, fulfilling requirements and pleasing the folks. The result is that many students arrive in classes, especially those on world politics, unable to find time to read, unable to comprehend what they read, and questioning if the class is relevant to their career plans. They opine that the world is too big and the concepts too abstract. This has led to questions of how to connect students' lives and hopes for a satisfying job with my hopes for a liberating educational experience for us both.

What is a liberating educational experience? I turn to ideas expressed by Paulo Freire in his two instructional books, *Pedagogy of the Oppressed* and *Pedagogy of Hope*. Both recommend that we share in the educational process by meeting students where they are, "and learning with them in community" (Schniedewind, 1987, 179). In

Friere's model, we are all students creating a *"co-intentional* education," including greater power sharing in the classroom and full participation of students in the structuring of their learning (Freire, 1970, 14).

Freire admonishes those of us who continue in the banking system, which he defines as education that becomes "an act of depositing, in which the students are depositories and the teacher is the depositor. Instead of communicating, the teacher issues communiqués and makes deposits which the students patiently receive, memorize, and repeat" (Freire, 1970, 58). In this system, class does not begin until the teacher arrives and then the students grab their pens to write down whatever they think they need to know; "Could you use an overhead please?" Many educators find tests and grades a distraction from the wonder of sharing knowledge and chafe under the pressure to clearly deliver examination material—in Freire's terms, banking. The tension is felt by all and most see the value of Freire's innovative work; however, even those of us who generally agree with Freire's method question how we, as banked teachers and students, in a banked system, can unbank pedagogy.

How can power be shared? I have asked for help from students in writing the syllabus, creating exams, and choosing the texts. The majority of the students like determining test format, but dislike selecting texts or writing the syllabus. I have always incorporated open discussion rather than prepared lectures, which allows students to 'read' and argue the texts from where they are and with each other. It allows the class to influence the direction of learning, which may be far afield of my anticipated trajectory. It also leaves the class vulnerable to a wasted hour. When students do not read and no lecture is forthcoming, there may be nothing to say. Liberation can be uncomfortable.

Are students interested in liberation? There is evidence that they are not. Some students request lectures and organization from the "only Ph.D. in the room" (student evaluation). Others question whether the professor is doing her or his job by asking students to participate in book selection, class discussion, or test writing. Although some students would like school to be different, most favor what they know. Banking is based on tradition, and, if it is not working, students tend to believe the teacher is not interesting or capable enough, the texts are poor choices, possibly too dense, or that other students have not studied enough. Very little thought is given to questioning the system (authority). In Freire's work on educating peasants in Brazil, there is lots of questioning of authority. In the United States, most students believe this is as good as it gets.

As a teacher, I am interested in unbanking my classes. Currently, I include discussion, video, guest speakers, games and theater as mechanisms for engaging students. This approach is not without critics. Some suggest that active learning panders to the television and computer age that many hold culpable for students' failure to learn. They argue that class activities and videos forfeit rigor and content. I argue that varying information delivery and experiential learning, if done well, motivates students to do the reading (and writing) so necessary to a successful liberal arts education. These activities allow students one more point of engagement with key ideas. They must take the ideas that experts present and move beyond the written word, the moving word (videos), and the teacher's word. That is the start of preparing students for a liberating life.

Finding activities that stimulate thinking about readings is a challenge. The activity needs to be creative enough to be playful, but not so creative that it is superficial. And one has to be prepared for the inevitable student who will find the activity "a waste of her or his time." One must trust that it is not, even when resistance to play is evident. As Walt Conley, an author in this text cleverly titled his chapter "Play to Learn," I could have titled my essay "Learn to Play."

The following two examples are efforts to pique students' curiosity enough so that they will want to read and become engaged in activities that illuminate some of the most important ideas we cover in the semester. The criteria for the selection of activities are: Does it focus on the course objectives? Does it create community within the classroom and beyond? (Do they talk about issues in the hallways?) Is what students learned shared among other students? (Are they teaching each other?) Finally, are students making the connection between theory and practice?

EXAMPLES OF EXPERIENTIAL LEARNING

Women and Politics: Let's Do Lunch

This idea was developed from a brief conversation at the Barbados Summer Institute on Curriculum Transformation, where a high school teacher and I started brainstorming about how to engage students in animating what they had read. That intention led to the idea of bringing together, at a luncheon, political women (and men who supported them) from the past and present. In the fall of 2001, I brought the idea to the students in the Women and Politics class.

The students cautiously agreed to the concept in principle, but only enthusiastically embraced it once I gave them a few simple guidelines and expectations. The assignment was to research a woman (or man if they could not bring themselves to "be" a woman), write a paper as a result of that research, and portray that person at a luncheon, which would be our final class together. The paper and the performance would constitute their final examination. I allowed each student to decide how much of their grade would be attributed to their paper and how much to their performance. This allowed flexibility for those students who have severe stage fright and cannot "perform." This also gave the students who have honed their speech skills rather than their writing skills the opportunity to demonstrate their learning through dramatic interpretation. It was agreed on by all, that this was a fair way to grade the final "exams."

The first stage was to create awareness of women in politics. For the first week of class I made several large name cards. On the cards I put various women's names. The list included an eclectic array of women, such as Empress Wu Chao, Rachel Carson, Rigoberta Menchu, Gro Harlem Bruntland, Catherine II of Russia, and Shirley Chisholm. Then I handed one card to each student and asked him or her to form a time line. They did not have to be exact, but maybe by decade? It was quite revealing. They did not know most of the people. For the next class they were to come prepared to teach their classmates about the person on the card. They did their homework, lined up correctly and then took a turn at the podium, telling us when the woman lived and why her name was on a card. This exercise revealed how much students did not know about women in history, sparking questions about *why* they did not know, fueling their interest in learning more.

Because this was a new endeavor and students were not sure what to do at the luncheon, I asked a graduate student in the English department to visit our class and give the Bella Abzug performance she had presented at a campus festival the previous spring. In about the third week of class, the student arrived at our door with a stunning orange hat, and began shaking hands and thanking students for gathering to hear her UN speech on women. The students loved her performance, and the fun and possibilities multiplied.

After that visit, students began actively searching for someone to research and reenact at our luncheon. I heard several conversations prior to class in which students shared ideas and asked each other for names. All students worried about whom to become, but the men were particularly stumped. They finally asked me who they might be and I, in turn, asked them to talk with professors in their major to see who the women activists (or men who supported women) were in their discipline. Two of the men were philosophy majors. They chose to portray Friedrich Engels and John S. Mill. The third male, a politics major, chose Frederick Douglass. The entire guest list included Geraldine Ferraro, Princess Diana, Mary Jones (Mother Jones), Eve Ensler, Hillary Rodham Clinton, Maya Angelou, Corazon Aquino, Sarah Moore Grimke, Queen Elizabeth I, Kathleen Kennedy Townsend, Virginia Wolf (me), and Karl Marx (faculty). The students chose the lunch menu, a ziti buffet, and sent out invitations to a few faculty members, asking them to join in the event and become a woman in politics or man who supported women. As you can see from the list, one faculty member participated, and two others came to the luncheon as observers, as did the president of the college.

Early in the semester we decided that if each person spoke for 3 to 5 minutes we would fill more than an hour. That seemed reasonable, although difficult. Some students complained that it was not enough time, while others fretted over how to fill their time. In the end, it proved both doable and adequate.

In the weeks before the luncheon, I called the chair of the drama department about helping with costumes. She was happy to assist and several students visited the drama department looking for clothes, wigs, and other props.

The costumes, research, and enthusiasm contributed to a great day for the Women and Politics class. The speeches were interesting and the students made the most of the event by wearing their costumes to other classes, sparking further discussion, and giving our classroom experiment campus-wide exposure. The trial run for the luncheon exceeded my expectations. Students defined the experience, they read books, and they taught us about one woman's (or man's) influence on our politics today.

The performance was the highlight of the year for many students and for me, too. It went better than I had hoped, and that was because of the students in the class—a strong core of women loved the idea and their enthusiasm was contagious. They would come to class and talk about how they were spending the day of the luncheon at the hairdresser and what they were reading. The momentum of the class was also enhanced by Hillary Clinton's visit to our campus midsemester. The class sat together and received special up-front seating at Hosmer Hall. We read *Madam President: Shattering the Glass Ceiling* first and had Hillary sign her chapter. This event was talked about for weeks and the students were proud to sit together and shake hands with a real woman in politics.

I will include the luncheon final again in the spring, with a few minor adjustments. The general outline will be the same, but rather than hold the luncheon as the last class, it will be the next-to-the-last class. This will allow us to reflect on the event together and also enable students to complete course evaluations that include comments on the luncheon.

Croquet: The Quad Becomes Our Gameboard

This second example is directly from an article titled "Teaching with a Mallet" by Sean Duffy. In this article, Duffy addresses a problem most teachers of international relations face: How can we help students get a handle on world politics when the gaps between system theories and practice appear to be a great abyss. The globe is an abstraction and so are politics. Therefore, teaching world politics can be especially stressful for students of politics.

In addition to the theory and practice disconnect, most students suffer from geography amnesia. They do not know where countries are located or how they were formed. Most students seem to think the current map is the way things have always been. Hence, they find world politics confusing, pedantic, and frustrating. It is always in flux. The challenge is to give students enough foundational knowledge to hang onto as they journey into the world of changing borders, governments, and ideologies. The hope is to generate political efficacy and an ongoing interest in active world citizenship.

Croquet has made a difference and helped achieve those objectives. Students are curious about how theory relates to the class and they want to understand foreign policy and newspaper headlines, so they are very interested in how croquet could possibly constitute a final exam in such a "tough" class. This little bit of curiosity helps move the class forward and what they discover is that the game models the complexity of the world in a relevant and fun way. It is theory and it is not, thus showing the weaknesses of even the most thoughtful theory to explain or predict the game of croquet, let alone world politics. Further, it applies at all levels of analysis, but seems especially useful in elucidating the link between personal and global issues. The game helps students think about who they are in the world and what their contribution to the world (game) might be.

The setup is easy. I choose a very public place on campus, the Quad, which is in the middle of the primary classroom buildings. I also choose to play it on the first beautiful day in the spring, rather than set a date. I inform students that they should not skip class on that first beautiful day because there is no way to make it up. One must experience it.

The day of the game I set up one croquet course and have two sets of mallets available. The first time I used croquet I preselected the teams because we were studying a difficult text, *Gendered World Politics*, and I wanted the game to help students experience gender theory. Hence, one team was all male, one team was all female, and the other teams were mixed. I announced the teams and then asked the students to select their color/ball. Each team was asked to designate their ball as a country. The all-male team chose to be the United States, the all-female team chose to be Iraq (remember, this was in the spring of 2001), and the other teams were the United Kingdom and Cuba. I told the students that since the international system is one of anarchy, I would not referee the game. They needed to work it out.

The first game began with lots of excitement and strategizing. The United States took an early lead and left all other teams several wickets behind. Then Iraq decided that since the United States was not paying any attention, they would cheat. They began by bypassing one wicket. No one noticed, but then they grew bolder, bypassing several. Other teams followed their lead. All teams, except the United States, began "cheating" with the result of catching up with the United States. When the United States realized what was happening they cried, "no fair, you can't do that," but no one listened and at that point the entire field became a rush for the final wicket. There was no longer any turn taking, just hitting the ball as quickly as possible to the end. It was a short game and they processed it a bit, but began serious discussion of rules when they were told they would play another game. The second game was much different. They took turns and no one cheated. It was a quieter, more organized game and seemed to be less fun for the students, but the contrast was instructive.

Aside from having a good time playing a game on a beautiful day, the students took the exercise home and thought about it. They came to the next class ready to discuss it. There they talked about what theories seemed most relevant and what it felt like to be in different positions on the field. They also discussed the internal (state) politics as well. Some teams blamed their poor performance on teammates, complaining that their team members did not take turns. Many said that they now understood why realism's construction of human nature was powerful, but incomplete.

I originally thought the final exam would have a short multiple-choice section and a long take-home essay on the game, but the students disagreed. They argued that each student should be able to determine the percentage/points attributed to each section of the exam. It was a great idea. It allowed those missing the activity to put all of their efforts into the multiple-choice section. The only caveat I made was that the minimum given to any section must be 10 percent.

I use this game every semester. Students look forward to playing croquet and each time it is slightly different. I still preselect teams and I remain out of the system while the game is in play. The general trend of a chaotic first game and more organized second is the norm. Last year, one student aptly observed that environment makes a big difference in behavior. Students act and speak differently when class is outside and takes place as a game—a lesson in game theory and diplomacy for that astute observer. He featured that premise in his essay and it was excellent. In fact, most of the essays were outstanding and revealed more learning than previous in-class exams. Students who knew their essay was good assigned 90 percent to it and they were generally correct. Grading was easy and it was the best semester I have had teaching world politics. The students learned the nuts and bolts of International Relations theory and applied them well.

CONCLUSION

Although I use several mechanisms to press students to read, share power, and become teachers, I fall short of Freire's hope for a liberating education. I have not yet figured out how students can fully participate in structuring their learning—that is, writing the syllabus and selecting texts. That has to be done prior to the beginning of the semester and there is something to be said for experience. I can more easily choose appropriate texts based on past experiences and feedback from students. To some extent, students influence these decisions, but not generally those currently in the class. Power sharing is also short-circuited by grades. I am the authority, I give the grades. This becomes an issue, primarily with "good" students. They know the banking system and they do well in it. They are often the first to complain about the worth of the class and the teacher when a co-intentional approach is used. Although we might expect that our best students are the ones who would embrace the method, more often they are driven by high marks. They are the most banked.

Other students, those who have adopted the "get by with doing the minimum," are often less frustrated by power sharing. In fact, some become intoxicated with the possibilities for free riding—designing a course that allows them maximum wiggle room. The majority, however, fall in the middle. At first they are skeptical, but then they find it is helpful. Many students comment that Women and Politics and World Politics were among "the best courses they have taken" and often mention the luncheon or croquet as highlights.

References

Duffy, Sean P. "Teaching with a Mallet: Conveying an Understanding of Systematic Perspectives on International Relations Intuitively—Croquet as Experiential Learning," in *International Studies Review* 2 no. 4 (November 2001): 384–400.

Freire, Paulo. *Pedagogy of the Oppressed*. New York: Continuum, 1970.

Freire, Paulo. *Pedagogy of Hope: Reliving Pedagogy of the Oppressed*. New York: Continuum, 1995.

Schniedewind, Nancy. "Feminist Values: Guidelines for Teaching Methodology in Women's Studies" in *Freire for the Classroom: A Sourcebook for Liberatory Teaching*, edited by Ira Shore. Portsmouth, NH: Boynton/Cook Publishers, 1987.

Tickner, J. Ann. *Gendering World Politics*. New York: Columbia University Press, 2001.

15

Play to Learn

Walter J. Conley
Biology

Learning is a word that attracts adjectives like a magnet. Constructive learning, inquiry learning, discovery learning, active learning, problem-based learning, service learning, cooperative learning, outcome-based learning, and project-based learning are some of the varieties that have been designed, researched and published. To someone new to this literature it might seem that there are many kinds of learning. But it is not learning that has many forms, but methods and techniques used to elicit it.
—Robert Leamnson 1999

Active learning is one of many "methods and techniques" that can assist students in learning difficult material and concepts. Methods and techniques used for learning are often misunderstood, resulting in a variety of definitions for each term. Active learning occurs when students are involved more than listening, or engaged in an activity (Bonwell and Eison, 1991). Students learn best when they are involved in the process and not passive recipients of information (Astin, 1985; Cross, 1987). Active learning can take many forms. The science laboratory is a classic example of active learning, when done well. But it is in the lecture hall that many leading educators are encouraging college faculty to lessen their dependence on formal lecture and include activities that engage students (Bonwell and Eison, 1991; NRC, 1996; Tobias, 1977).

Play, as a mechanism for active learning in college, is infrequently used (Reiber 1996), even though there is evidence for the benefits of play (Grechus and Brown, 2000; Ingram, 1998). Reiber, (1996) suggested that early childhood play is critical in psychological, social, and intellectual development. Although difficult to define, clearly there is a strong connection between playing and learning (Kuczaj, 1998; Provost, 1990). Play can help take the stress out of learning a particularly difficult concept (Davison, 1984). At the same time, play promotes group work that can result in high levels of enthusiasm (Cloke, 1987).

But children play and adults leisure (Chick and Barnett, 1995). The adult educational profession has been ambivalent toward the value of games as a learning tool—many in higher education regard play as the opposite of work, and thus of little or no value (Reiber, 1996). On the other hand, less formal corporate and military training facilities embrace the use of simulations and games as instructional tools (Greenblat, 1987; Greenblat and Duke, 1981).

EXAMPLES OF PLAY TO LEARN

The following two examples of active learning address two ends of the continuum of energy transfer among organisms, photosynthesis, and food webs. Transfer of energy, from photosynthesis to food webs, is one of the major themes in life science (AAAS, 1990 1993; NRC, 1996). Photosynthesis is often described as the most important chemical equation known (Campbell et al., 2003), but one of the most difficult concepts for students to grasp. The devil is in the details. The first example is a play that is acted out in the lecture hall. The second example is a card game developed to demonstrate many of the nuances of trophic transfer.

Many lecture halls have stadium-type seating. Usually designed to accommodate 100 to 300 students, these halls are perfect for this type of play. The photosynthesis play evolved from a simple classroom demonstration. In an effort to display how electrons transfer energy in electron transport chains, a small ball was thrown to someone at the back of the room. The student was instructed to roll the ball down the stairs (see also Cornerly, 1999). The demonstration included a discussion of kinetic and potential energy plus enzyme function in electron transport chains. Although the idea of expanding this simple demonstration into a more elaborate play had been "bouncing around" in my head for some time, it took a special class of receptive students to provide the catalyst. This first example includes the entire set of instructions and background information that were provided to students.

EXAMPLE 1: PLAYING WITHIN CHLOROPLASTS
PHOTOSYNTHESIS TRANSFERS RADIANT ENERGY
INTO CHEMICAL ENERGY

Photosynthesis captures and then transfers solar energy
to organic molecules.

Often described as the most significant chemical reaction on the planet, photosynthesis captures the energy of packets of light (PHOTONS) and converts that energy to a form that can be used by cells by making sugars (SYNTHESIS). With the exception of some deep-sea vent communities, earth's ecosystems depend upon photosynthesis for energy. Organisms that derive their energy from inorganic sources are referred to as autotrophs (= self feeding). Organisms that feed on autotrophs are called heterotrophs (= other feeding).

The equation for photosynthesis provides a summary of the materials required and the products of the reaction:

$$6CO_2 + 12H_2O \xrightarrow{\text{SUN}} C_6H_{12}O_6 + 6O_2 + 6H_2O$$

Photosynthesis requires carbon dioxide, water, and sunlight. The products are oxygen, water, and simple sugars like glucose.

Eukaryotic photosynthesis occurs within chloroplasts. Chloroplasts are most abundant within cells of leaves, but are also in other green parts of plants. Specific structures within chloroplasts house the required pigments for photosynthesis. These structures, called thylakoids, are flattened membranous compartments arranged in stacks called grana (granum is the singular). The fluid part of the chloroplast is called the stroma.

Photosynthesis occurs in two stages

The word "photosynthesis" captures the two stages or pathways. The first stage uses light energy or photons and these reactions are called the light-dependent reactions. Water is split and electrons are moved from a low- to a high-energy state. Oxygen gas is produced in this step. In other words, kinetic energy from photons (particles of light traveling at great speeds) is transferred to electrons in the photopigments of chlorophyll and other molecules. Transfer raises electrons to higher energy levels as they are transferred to electron acceptor molecules. The energy of these electrons is passed through a series of reactions, each one lowering the energy a small step in an electron transport chain. This energy is used to move protons (hydrogen ions) across chloroplast membranes, setting up for chemiosmosis. Chemiosmosis then makes ATP. A second similar set of reactions occurs that produces a different high-energy molecule, NADPH.

In summary, the first step uses the energy from the sun, plus water, to transfer and store energy in the molecules ATP and NADPH. Oxygen gas is produced as a waste product.

The second stage of photosynthesis is the synthesis stage because sugar molecules are synthesized. These are the light-independent reactions. The second stage includes a complex set of cyclic reactions called the Calvin Cycle. The energy supplied in the bonds of ATP and NADPH is transferred into the bonds of glucose or other sugars. The carbon used to make the sugars comes from atmospheric carbon dioxide.

In summary, the second stage transfers the energy from the bonds of ATP and NADPH to sugars, creating complex organic molecules from the gas CO_2.

Making Connections

The photosynthetic process has enormous global significance. The entire ecology of our planet revolves around the flow of energy from the sun through photosynthesis to cellular respiration. Because plants use CO_2 to build their organic molecules (recall that organic chemistry is centered around the carbon atom), the bulk of the weight of any plant comes from thin air. Therefore, because our bulk carbon and mass are based on the photosynthetic process, we are also creatures created from thin air.

ACT ONE: THE LIGHT-DEPENDENT REACTIONS
aka THE LIGHT REACTIONS
PHOTO

Scene One: Photosystem II

The Role of Water

Water is one of the required materials for photosynthesis. Two molecules of water split, producing as a waste product oxygen gas or O_2. The remaining hydrogen atoms join the chlorophyll within the chloroplast.

The Role of Sunlight

Light has both wave and particle properties. When the packet of energy or photons from sunlight interacts with the pigments of chlorophyll, the molecules become "excited." Eventually, the electrons from the water molecule are raised to a higher energy level when they are transferred within the chloroplast to an electron acceptor.

Electron Transport Chain

Explosive release of energy is not efficient. To efficiently transfer energy from the high-energy electrons, they are passed through a series of membrane proteins. As the membrane proteins use the energy of the "falling" electrons, they pump hydrogen ions across the membrane. This sets up a concentration gradient of H+ on one side of the membrane. The enzyme ATP synthase uses the energy of this concentration gradient to create a bond by joining ADP and P to form ATP.

Summary

During this stage of photosynthesis light and water, interacting with the chlorophyll pigments, raise electrons to higher levels. "Falling" electrons transfer their energy to making the bonds of ATP molecules.

Scene Two: Photosystem I
The Role of Sunlight

Light also interacts with the chlorophyll pigments of this photosystem, although their wavelength of peak absorbance is different. When the packet of energy or photons from sunlight interacts with the pigments of chlorophyll, the molecules become "excited." Eventually, electrons from Photosystem II are raised to a higher level when they are transferred from chlorophyll to an electron acceptor.

Electron Transport Chain

Explosive release of energy is not efficient. To efficiently transfer energy from the high-energy electrons, they are passed through a series of membrane proteins. A different type of high-energy molecule is made during this stage of photosynthesis, NADPH.

Summary

At the end of the light-dependent reactions, light energy has been transferred to the bonds of two high-energy molecules, ATP and NADPH.

These molecules are used in the next stage of photosynthesis, the light-independent reactions.

ACT TWO: THE LIGHT-INDEPENDENT REACTIONS
aka THE DARK REACTIONS
SYNTHESIS

Scene One: The Source of Carbon

The source of carbon that finds its way into the organic molecules originates as "stardust." Carbon is formed when stars die, or go supernova. The "dust" from these explosions makes its way through space onto distant planets. The inorganic source of carbon on earth is atmospheric carbon or CO_2.

Scene Two: The Calvin Cycle

Carbon Dioxide (CO_2) enters a series of cyclic reactions during this part of photosynthesis. The high-energy molecules from the light dependent reactions, ATP and NADPH, transfer their bond energy to make glucose from inorganic carbon.

WHAT YOU DO

Your assignment is to develop a dialogue for your group and assign roles to each member. Your instructor will separate the class into functional groups based on the photosynthetic process. Your instructor will also provide all of the props. The dialogue that will be developed by your group will be a short script that explains to the class your role in the photosynthetic process. You can use cue cards and must do some research using your text and the Internet resources provided at the end of this handout. Suggestions regarding the topics you may include in your script are provided in the following instructions.

Photosystem II

This group must dress in green. You might want to practice being "excited" when light shines on the chloroplast.
    Consider the following questions when preparing your script.
- What is the dominant pigment in this photosystem? What are some of the accessory pigments and what wavelengths do they absorb? What is the function of the accessory pigments?
- Why is this called Photosystem II if it is the first to act?
- What is P680?
- How can molecules become excited?

The Role of Water

This group will be provided with squirt guns. Watch out, chloroplasts!
Consider the following questions when preparing your script.
- What part of the water molecule donates electrons to the
  photosystem?
- What is the waste product of this reaction?
- What is the ecological, or global, significance of the produc-
  tion of this "waste"?

The Role of Sunlight

This group will be provided with flashlights. The concept here is a diffi-
cult one.
Consider the following questions when preparing your script.
- What is electromagnetic energy?
- What are the wavelengths of this energy that are absorbed by
  the chloroplasts of plants?
- What is the nature of photons?

First Electron Transport Chain

This group will be provided with small balls that represent the "electrons" that will be transported from the back of the room to the front
(down the steps). You must select a member from your group to act as
the primary electron acceptor. Three other members of the group will
represent ATP molecules.
Consider the following questions when preparing your script.
- Why is it important for cells to shuttle energy through steps?
- What are the ions that are moved across the membrane
  during electron transport?
- What enzyme facilitates the movement of ions back across
  membranes, thus creating ATP?
- What is the role of oxygen during similar electron transport
  reactions of cellular respiration?
- What is the product of these reactions?

Photosystem I

This group also must dress in green. You might want to practice
being "excited" when light shines on the chloroplast. Consider the following questions when preparing your script.

- What is the dominant pigment in this photosystem? What are some of the accessory pigments and what are their colors? What is the function of the accessory pigments?
- Why is this called Photosystem I if it is the second to act?
- What is P700?
- How can molecules become excited?

Second Electron Transport Chain

This group will also be provided with small balls that represent the "electrons" that will be transported from the back of the room to the front (down the steps). You must select a primary electron acceptor. Three other members of the group will represent NADPH molecules.

Consider the following questions when preparing your script.
- Why is it important for cells to shuttle energy through steps?
- What are the ions that are moved across the membrane during electron transport?
- What is the enzyme that facilitates the movement of the ions back across the membrane, creating ATP?
- What is the role of oxygen during similar electron transport reactions of cellular respiration?
- What is the product of these reactions?

The Source of Carbon

This group should practice some deep exhales.

Consider the following questions when preparing your script.
- What is the source of carbon, both recent and ancient?
- If a plant grows from a seedling weighing 1 gram to a mighty oak of several hundred kilograms, what is source of the bulk of the dry weight of the plant?
- Biologists argue that we are creatures created from thin air. Please explain this reference.

The Calvin Cycle

This is a cyclic reaction so this group will be walking in circles. Cookies or candy, filled with glucose molecules, will be provided by your instructor for distribution.

Consider the following questions when preparing your script.
- What is the source of energy that is transferred into the bonds of glucose?

- How do cells use the glucose molecules that are a result of photosynthesis?
- Are any other molecule types produced during this process?

EXAMPLE 2: TRANSFER OF ENERGY WITHIN AQUATIC COMMUNITIES TROPHIC PYRAMIDS —WHAT'S IN THE CARDS?

Details of the food web game are described elsewhere (Conley, 2004). While recognizing the subtleties and complexities of trophic transfer (Conley and Turner, 1985; Turner and Roff, 1993), the game was designed as a simplified version of energy transfer within aquatic communities. What follows is a descriptive account of student activities during the game.

The initial target group included students in a marine biology class for nonmajors, but the game has been used successfully in upper-level classes for biology majors as well. In each case, students are provided background information by lecture and/or reading assignments on trophic transfer of energy. This background information provides students a first look at the characters (e.g., diatoms, dinoflagellates, copepods, etc.) that are on the cards. Each group of four to five students is given a deck of cards. Prizes are announced up front with enough prizes (textbooks, CDs, movie tickets) to encourage friendly competition and enhanced attention to the game. The idea is to incorporate the information students learn about food webs and local organisms into trophic pyramids.

Most cards relate to a trophic level. Additional cards are needed to start the game. Each card includes some text that explains the "fit" of the card in the pyramid. The cards include:
- The sun card, with nutrients, sunlight, and CO_2, the materials needed for photosynthesis.
- Primary producers—phytoplankton. This is a nearshore pelagic example; thus, diatoms and dinoflagellates are the dominant forms.
- Primary consumers—zooplankton. Copepods and krill are the most numerous herbivores within nearshore marine aquatic communities.
- Secondary consumers. Most zooplanktivorous animals are smaller silver-bodied fishes like anchovies, sardines, and herring (forage or bait fishes).

- Tertiary consumers are, for the most part, fishes that eat other fishes. Snook and grouper are common tropical-sub-tropical examples.
- Top predators include sharks, marlin, tuna, swordfish, and humans.

Each player is dealt five cards that are held in their hand. The remainder of the deck is placed face down in the middle of the players. Each player takes a turn, but no player can begin the pyramid play until a "Required Resources" card is played (requirements for photosynthesis).

All pyramids start with primary producers, as phytoplankton, and flows through zooplankton to fishes and other organisms.

During a player's turn, the player either plays a card placing it on the table face up, or draws from the deck and passes. Only connections listed on the cards can be made. Each new layer (trophic level) within a pyramid will have one less card than the layer below. For example, it would take six phytoplankton cards to support five zooplankton cards. A pyramid is not complete until the top carnivore is played. This is a "winner take all" game. The player who places the top carnivore takes the pyramid and accumulates the points of the cards. These cards are then shuffled back into the deck. At the end of the game (when time is up), scores are tallied and prizes awarded.

DISCUSSION

Can play enhance learning? Students perceive a strong connection between play and social development, and a general relation between play and learning (Edgar, 1996). Among other animals, play is most often associated with social bonding (Caro, 1988; Fagen, 1995). In fact, absence of play has been associated with pathological behavior among primates (Goodall, 1986, 1990). Although there are risks involved (Harcourt, 1991), behaviorists have long recognized the role of play in learning among a variety of mammals (Fagen, 1995). Feline cubs establish dominance hierarchy and practice essential hunting and stalking skills while playing with siblings. Play behavior in rats assists in the development of behaviors essential to their self-defense (Einon and Potegal, 1991; Potegal and Einon, 1989). But clearly, cetaceans and primates display the most complex forms of play. Evidence of play as a tool to learn is also strongest among these animals (Brown, 1988; Goodall, 1986; McCowan et al., 2000). For recent review of animal play, see Burghardt (2005).

The most frequently encountered examples of play to learn in college are the use of a variety of games, especially within colleges of business (Delemeester and Brauer, 2000; Greenlaw and Wyman, 1973; Wolfe, 1985). Among the sciences, health science professionals have successfully employed card and board games as well as computer-based simulations in their curriculum (Ball, 2000; Ingram et al., 1998; Wargo, 2000; Youseffi et al., 2000). Chemists are surprisingly playful, incorporating acting (Cornerly, 1999), cards (Granath and Russell, 1999), board games (Edmonson and Lewis, 1999; Russell 1999), arcade games (Garcia-Ruiz, 1999) puzzles and conundrums (Castro-Acuna et al., 1999; DeLorenzo, 1999; Helser, 2000; Rybolt and Waddell, 1999), and popular formats such as Jeopardy (Keck, 2000) and BINGO (Crute, 2000; Mauter, 1999; Tejada and Palacios, 1995). A number of games are commercially available (see Russell, 1999 for vendor contact information).

Can adult play enhance learning in college? Professional attitudes about play are polarized (Barber and Norman, 1989). Supporters focus on the fact that play provides enjoyment and enhanced interest in the topic. Interest provides motivation, which is a key component to learning (Astin, 1985; Bonwell and Eison, 1991; Cross, 1987). The attributes of play are similar to the self-rewarding activities contained within modern educational theory (Kolesnick, 1970; Reiber, 1996). By being part of the experience, students are not the passive recipients of information that research shows reduces attention (Bonwell and Eison, 1991). When learning is fun, it is more effective (Lepper and Cordova, 1992). Glickman, (1984) argues that play offers long-term benefits, providing intellectual and social growth for many years. Detractors of play learning consider the practice trendy, frivolous, and inadequately evaluated (Barber and Norman, 1989).

The benefits of many activities are difficult to measure and much of the feedback to faculty is often anecdotal. Student surveys reveal that in-class activities are always among the most favorably received learning resources (Bonwell and Eison, 1991). Whereas many authors have suggested that there are learning benefits from the use of games and other forms of play, few conclusive studies document enhanced learning (Grechus and Brown, 2000; Greenlaw and Wyman, 1973; Wolf, 1985). Cessario (1987) evaluated a self-designed board game for nursing theory. Students who played the game in addition to classroom instruction performed significantly better on a standardized test. Students in health sciences also gained significant long-term learning benefits from game play (Ingram et al., 1998). The more times the game was played, the higher the score on post-tests. Thus, the use of games as a reinforcement of information has demonstrated significant benefits (Grechus and Brown, 2000). Well-designed games may best be used as a supplement to traditional forms of teaching (Ingram et al., 1998).

Whenever a game or play is used to reinforce a concept, a large percentage of the students mention them as the best leaning experience of the semester. The two activities described here were most recently used in a nonmajors biology section for elementary education majors. The course is activity rich, with over thirty separate assigned activities ranging from on-line and CD assignments, student-designed experiments, wet labs, and game play. In an end-of-semester survey, 92 percent of the students identified one of the two energy transfer games as the activity that best helped them understand a difficult concept. But student perceptions may not reflect reality. The learning benefits of these activities require further testing—it was difficult not to conduct the activity because of the positive response from students. The second semester of "nonplay" was during the fall of 2006 and these data will be used to assess the learning benefits from these activities.

REFERENCES

American Association for the Advancement of Science. *Science for All Americans: Project 2061*. New York: Oxford University Press, 1990.

American Association for the Advancement of Science. *Benchmarks for Science Literacy: Project 2061*. New York: Oxford University Press, 1993.

Astin, A. W. *Achieving Educational Excellence*. San Francisco: Josey-Bass, 1985.

Ball, K. S. "Anatomy and Physiology: Games We Play." *Nurse Educator* 25 (2000): 156.

Barber, P., and I. Norman. "Preparing Teachers for the Performance and Evaluation of Gaming-Simulation in Experiential Learning Climates." *Journal of Advanced Nursing* 14 (1989): 146–151.

Bonwell, C. C., and J. A. Eison. "Active Learning: Creating Excitement in the Classroom." *ASHE—ERIC Higher Education Reports* 1 (1991): 1–104.

Brown, S. G. "Play Behavior in Lowland Gorillas: Age Differences, Sex Differences, and Possible Functions." *Primates* 29 (1988): 219–228.

Burghardt, G. M.. *The Genesis of Animal Play: Testing the Limits*. Cambridge: MIT Press, 2005.

Campbell, N. A, J. R. Reese, L. G. Mitchell, and M. R. Taylor. *Biology: Concepts & Connections,* 4th ed, San Francisco: Benjamin Cummings, 2003.

Caro, T. M. "Adaptive Significance of Play: Are We Getting Closer?" *Trends in Ecology and Evolution* 3 (1988): 50–53.

Castro-Acuña, C. M., R. E. Dominguez-Danache, P. B. Kelter, and V. Grundman. "Puzzles in Chemistry and Logic." *Journal of Chemical Education* 76 (1999): 496–498.

Cessario, L. Utilization of Board Gaming for Conceptual Models of Nursing. 26 (1987): 167–169.

Chick, G., and L. A. Barnett. "Children Play and Adults Leisure." In A. D. Pellegrini, Ed., *The Future of Play Theory: A Multidisciplinary Inquiry into the Contributions of Brian Sutton-Smith* (pp. 45–69). Albany: State University of New York Press, 1995.

Chimeno, J. "How to Make Learning Chemical Nomenclature Fun, Exciting, and Palatable." *Journal of Chemical Education* 77 (2000): 144–145.

Cloke, P. "Applied Rural Geography and Planning: A Simple Gaming Technique." *Journal of Geography in Higher Education* 11 (1987): 35–45.

Conley, W. J. "Eating Sunlight: From the Sun Through the Sea." In: R. L. Potter and G. G. Meisels, Eds. *Science That Matters,* vol. 2, pp. 127–187. Dubuque, Iowa: Kendall Hunt, 2004.

Conley, W. J. and J. T. Turner. "Omnivory by Two Coastal Marine Copepods, Centropages Hamatus and Labidocera Aestiva." *Marine Ecology Progress Series* 21 (1985): 113–120.

Cornerly, K. "The Electron Transport Game." *Biochemical Education* 27 (1999): 74–76.

Cross, K. P. "Teaching for Learning." *AAHE Bulletin* 39 (1987): 3–7.

Crute, T. D. "Classroom Nomenclature Games—BINGO." *Journal of Chemical Education* 77 (2000): 481–482.

Davison, J. G. "Real Tears: Using Role Plays and Simulations." *Curriculum Review* 23 (1984): 91–94.

Deavor, J. P. "Chemical Jeopardy." *Journal of Chemical Education* 73 (1996): 430.

Delemeester, G., and J. Brauer. "Games Economists Play: Noncomputerized Classroom Games." *Journal of Chemical Education* 31 (2000): 406.

DeLorenzo, D. "When Hell Freezes Over: An Approach to Develop Student Interest and Communication Skills." *Journal of Chemical Education* 76 (1999): 503.

Edgar, K. "The Value of Play as Perceived by Wheelock College Freshman." In: *Playin for Keeps: Supporting Children's Play: Topics in Early Childhood Education.* 1996. Phillips, A. L. (ed). St. Paul MN: Redleaf Press.

Edmonson, L. J., and D. L. Lewis. "Equilibrium Principles: a Game for Students." *Journal of Chemical Education* 76 (1999): 502.

Einon, D., and M. Potegal. "Enhanced Defense in Adult Rats Deprived of Playfighting Experience in Juveniles." *Aggressive Behavior* 17 (1991): 27–46.

Fagen, R. "Animal Play, Games of Angels, Biology, and Brain." In A. D. Pellegrini, Ed., *The Future of Play Theory: A Multidisciplinary Inquiry into the Contributions of Brian Sutton-Smith,* (pp. 23–44). Albany: State University of New York Press, 1995.

Garcia-Ruiz, J. M. "Arcade Games for Teaching Crystal Growth." *Journal of Chemical Education* 76 (1999): 499–501.

Geiger, B. F. "Using Eco-Bingo to Teach Students about Environmental Health and Safety Education." *Journal of Health Education* 31 (2000): 118–119.

Glickman, C. D. "Play in Public School Settings: A Philosophical Question." In T. D. Yawkey and A. D. Pellegrini, Eds., *Child's Play: Developmental and Applied,* (pp. 255–271). Hillsdale, NJ: Erlbaum, 1984.

Goodall, J. *The Chimpanzees of Gombe.* Cambridge: Belknap Press, 1986.

Goodall, J. *Through a Window: My Thirty Years with the Chimpanzees of Gombe.* Boston: Houton Mifflin, 1990.

Granath, P. L., and J. V. Russell. "Using Games to Teach Chemistry. 1. The Old Prof Card Game." *Journal of Chemical Education* 76 (1999): 485–486.

Grechus, M., and J. Brown. "Comparison of Individualized Computer Game Reinforcement versus Peer-Interactive Board Game Reinforcement on Retention of Nutrition Label Knowledge." *Journal of Health Education* 31 (2000): 138–142.

Greenblat, C. S. *Designing Games and Simulations: An Illustrated Handbook.* Newbury Park, CA: Sage, 1987.

Greenblat, C. S., and R. D. Duke. *Principles and Practices of Gaming-Simulation.* Beverly Hills: Sage, 1981.

Greenlaw, P. S., and F. P. Wyman. "The Teaching Effectiveness of Games in Collegiate Business Courses." *Simulation and Games* 4 (1973): 259–294.

Harcourt, R. "Survivorship Costs of Play in the South American Fur Seal." *Animal Behavior* 42 (1991): 509–511.

Helser, T. L. "Sugar Wordsearch." *Journal of Chemical Education* 77 (2000): 480.

Ingram, C., K. Ray, and J. Landeen. "Evaluation of an Educational Game for Health Sciences Students." *Journal of Nursing Education* 37 (1998): 240–246.

Jones, A. G., J. Jasperson, and D. Gusa. "Cranial Nerve Wheel of Competencies." *Journal of Continuing Education in Nursing* 31 (2000): 152–154.

Keck, M. V. "A Final Exam Review Activity Based on the Jeopardy Format." *Journal of Chemical Education* 77 (2000): 483.

Kolesnik, W. B. *Educational Psychology.* New York: McGraw Hill, 1970.

Kuczaj, S. A. "Is an Evolutionary Theory of Language Play Possible?" *Current Psychology of Cognition* 17 (1998): 135–154.

Leamnson, R. *Thinking About Teaching and Learning: Developing Habits of Learning with First Year College and University Students.* Sterling, VA: Stylus, 1999.

Lepper, M. R., and D. I. Cordova. "A Desire to be Taught: Instructional Consequences of Intrinsic Motivation." *Motivation and Emotion* 16 (1992): 187–208.

Mauter, L. "Periodic Table Bingo." *Science Scope* 22 (1999): 32.

McCowan, B., L. Marino, E. Vance, L. Walke, and D. Reiss. "Bubble Ring Play of Bottlenose Dolphins (Tursiops truncatus): Implications for Cognition." *Journal of Comparative Psychology* 114 (2000): 98–106.

National Research Council (NRC). *National Science Education Standards.* Washington, DC: National Academy Press, 1996.

Potegal, M., and D. Einon. "Aggressive Behavior in Adult Rats Deprived of Playfighting Experience in Juveniles." *Developmental Psychobiology* 22 (1989): 159–172.

Provost, J. A. *Work, Play, and Type: Achieving Balance in Your Life.* Palo Alto, CA: Consulting Psychologist Press, 1990.

Reiber, L. P. "Seriously Considering Play: Designing Interactive Learning Environments Based on the Blending of Microworlds, Simulations, and Games." *Educational Technology, Research, and Development* 44 (1996): 43–58.

Russell, J. V. "Using Games to Teach Chemistry: an Annotated Bibliography." *Journal of Chemical Education* 76 (1999): 481–144.

Rybolt, T. R., and T. G. Waddell. "The Chemical Adventures of Sherlock Holms: The Death Puzzle at 212B Baker Street." *Journal of Chemical Education* 76 (1999): 489–493.

Tejada, S., and J. Palacios. "Chemical Elements Bingo." *Journal of Chemical Education* 72 (1995): 1115–1116.

Tobias, S. *Revitalizing Undergraduate Science: Why Some Things Work and Most Don't.* Tucson, AZ: Research Cooperation, 1977.

Turner, J. T., and J. C. Roff. "Trophic Levels and Trophospecies in Marine Plankton: Lessons from the Microbial Food Web." *Marine Microbial Food Webs* 7 (1993): 225–248.

Wargo, C. A. "Blood Clot: Gaming to Reinforce Learning about Disseminated Intravascular Coagulation." *The Journal of Continuing Education in Nursing* 31 (2000): 149–151.

Whitman, V. L., and M. Nielsen. An Experiment to Evaluate Drama as a Method for Teaching Social Work Research. *Journal of Social Work Education* 22 (1986): 31–42.

Wolfe, J. "The Teaching Effectiveness of Games in Collegiate Business Courses: A 1973–1983 Update." *Simulation and Games* 16 (1985): 251–288.

Youseffi, F., R. Caldwell, and P. Hadnot. "Recall Rummy: Learning Can be Fun." *The Journal of Continuing Education in Nursing* 31 (2000): 161–162.

List of Contributors

Sergei Abramovich, Professor of Mathematics Education at the Department of Early Childhood, Childhood and General Professional Education (primary appointment) and the Department of Secondary Education (secondary appointment), came to SUNY Potsdam in 1998. Since then, he has been a teacher to some 2,000 prospective teachers of mathematics. His current research interests span across K–16 mathematics education with particular emphasis on the appropriate use of technology in the development of mathematical concepts, both elementary and advanced.

Robert L. Badger has taught geology at SUNY Potsdam since 1989. His research involves the geochemistry of some 570-million-year-old volcanic rocks in the Blue Ridge Mountains of Shenandoah National Park in Virginia, and their correlative igneous rocks in the Adirondack region of northern New York. He has published a layman's guide to the geology of Shenandoah National Park, and is currently working on a similar guidebook for the Adirondack Park of northern New York.

Lawrence P. Brehm, currently a faculty member of the Physics Department at SUNY Potsdam, has taught physics, mathematics, and biology at the secondary and college levels, and worked in the computer industry in the areas of fiber-optic communications hardware and systems, electronics packaging, and component reliability. His research interests include optical metrology, physical methods applied to biological problems, and information.

Peter S. Brouwer is currently Professor of Secondary Mathematics Education and Coordinator of the Secondary Mathematics Education program at SUNY Potsdam, where he has worked since 1980. He has also served in a variety of administrative positions, including provost of the college from 1996–2000, and as a faculty member in computer science. He has been recognized with awards for excellence in teaching at both the college and state levels. His current research relates to the role of technology in mathematical problem solving.

Walter J. Conley started his research career at the Florida Marine Research Institute and his research interests include trophic interaction within aquatic communities, with a focus on the feeding of zooplankton. He has been teaching college and university life sciences for over twenty years, and is currently conducting research on the effects of class size and various classroom activities on student learning.

David Curry has been teaching philosophy at SUNY Potsdam since 1990 after receiving his Ph.D. from the University of Virginia. An historian of philosophy by training, his research explores Plato's metaphysics and epistemology, while his teaching ranges across the whole spectrum of philosophical inquiry.

Caroline Downing is Professor of Art History at SUNY Potsdam, specializing in Greek and Roman art and archaeology. A former director of the Interdisciplinary Learning Communities Program, she is the recipient of the Distinguished Honors Professor of the Year Award and the President's Award for Excellence in Teaching.

Joel Foisy has enjoyed teaching first-year through master's level mathematics courses at SUNY Potsdam since 1996. For many summers, he has served as a faculty advisor in an NSF-sponsored Research Experience for Undergraduates, working with students on problems in topological graph theory.

William E. Herman earned his doctorate at the University of Michigan and has taught at SUNY Potsdam for the last fourteen years of his twenty-nine years of full-time university teaching experience. His current research interests include the improved translation of the psychological knowledge base into professional practice, motivational dispositions, moral development, and test anxiety.

John Massaro is SUNY Distinguished Teaching Professor of Politics at SUNY Potsdam. He has published, *Supremely Political: The Role of Ideology and Presidential Management in Unsuccessful Supreme Court Nominations* (SUNY Press, 1990) and his articles have appeared in both scholarly and popular journals. He teaches courses in U.S. politics and public law as well as courses focusing on Bruce Springsteen and politics and the politics of basketball.

Galen Pletcher has been Dean of Arts and Sciences at SUNY Potsdam since 1994. He teaches comparative religion and philosophy of religion on a regular basis. He has published in the fields of philosophy of religion, ethics, and philosophy of science. He has recently begun teaching a class for first-year students on the varying conceptions of human nature.

Oscar Sarmiento has taught Latin American literature and culture and Spanish for thirteen years at SUNY Potsdam. His research involves Latin American contemporary poetry, deconstruction, translation, and gender studies. He is a contributing editor to the *Handbook of Latin American Studies*.

Heather Sullivan-Catlin is Associate Professor of Sociology with a focus on social movements, gender, community and environmental sociology, and experiential learning. She is active in developing service-learning pedagogy at the campus, state, and national levels.

Liliana Trevizán, an Associate professor of Modern Languages, has taught Spanish, Latin American Literature, and Women's Studies classes at SUNY Potsdam for fifteen years. Her research explores the writing of Latin American women on politics and sexuality, as well as the discourse(s) of democracy.

Peg Wesselink earned her PhD in political science at the University of Iowa and has taught at the University of South Florida, SUNY Potsdam, and the University of Sinaloa in Culican, Mexico. Her work examines international political economy, feminism, and the media. She is currently residing in Gulfport, Florida.

Ronald Woodbury served in various roles from college professor to college president at five colleges and universities over a thirty-year academic career from which he retired in 2001. He helped pioneer learning communities and active learning strategies as a faculty member and administrator at Evergreen State College in Olympia, Washington, and as Vice President for Academic Affairs at SUNY Potsdam. An extensive record of articles, presentations, and workshops testifies to his on-going interest in helping other colleges and universities shape innovation to a variety of academic structures and traditions. He is currently residing in St. Augustine, Florida.

Index

Abramovich, Sergei, 93, 163
Abzug, Bella, 140
academic expectations, 37
achievement: personal, 21
active learning, 147–48
active unlearning, 69–70, 72, 73–74
Adirondack Great Camps, 53
Adirondack Museum at Blue
  Mountain Lake, x, 53
Adirondack Studies Program, xiv,
  39n, 51–55, 61–62
adulthood, 25
alienation: in adolescence, 21–22
All about My Mother (Pedro
  Almódovar), 32
Allende, Isabel, (*Daughter of
  Fortune*), 31, 33
Almódovar, Pedro, (*All about My
  Mother*), 32
"American Skin (41 shots)," 27
anthropology: department of, 39n
Anzaldúa, Gloria, (*Making
  Faces/Haciendo Caras*), 31
Apology (Socrates), 71
architecture: Adirondack, 53; south-
  west, 55
Aristotle, 116
art: department of, 51; history,
  51–55; landscape, 51–55; studio,
  51–55
Asimov, Isaac, 124
assessment: institutional, 11
Astin, Alexander, 87

At Home in the Universe (John
  Wheeler), 118

Badger, Robert, vii, 57, 163
"Badlands," 21, 23, 24
Bak, Per (*How Nature Works*), xi
Baker, Sheridan (*The Practical
  Stylist*), 89
Baldwin, Brewster, xiv
Barbados Summer Institute, 139
BC Comics, 64
Benjamin, Walter, 79
Berger, Peter (*Invitation to
  Sociology*), 9, 16
Beyond the Culture Wars (Gerald
  Graff), 78
biology: department of, 147; teaching
  and learning of, 147–58
border crossing, 29, 30, 31, 32, 33,
  35, 38
"Born in the USA," 20
"Born to Run," 21, 22, 23
boundaries: disciplinary, 29
brainstorming, 90
Brehm, Lawrence, 105, 163
Brouwer, Peter, xi, 41, 163
business environment, 42

calculus, SEE mathematics
Call of Service, The (Robert Coles),
  13–14
Calvin Cycle, 150, 152, 154
Castillo, Debra, ("Border Crossing:
  Mexico/USA,"), 35, 39n

167